GOD IN CARTOONS

Other Books by Mark Bryant

World War II in Cartoons

The Complete Colonel Blimp (ed.)

The Comic Cruikshank (ed.)

Vicky's Supermac (ed.)

Dictionary of British Cartoonists & Caricaturists 1730–1980 (with S. Heneage)

GOD IN
CARTOONS

Mark Bryant

Highland Books

First published in England in 1997
by Highland Books Ltd,
2 High Pines, Knoll Rd, Godalming, Surrey GU7 2EP

ISBN 1 897913 38 9

Printed and bound by Caledonian International Book
Manufacturing, Glasgow

Front cover illustration by Noel Ford
Back cover cartoon by Peter Maddocks

For Robert, Jane and Charlotte

Contents

Acknowledgements viii

1. Old Testament Tales 1

2. Heaven and Hell 15

3. The Life of Jesus 27

4. Saints and Sinners 39

5. Rules and Rites 51

6. Festivals and Holy Days 63

7. Monks and Nuns 71

8. The Clergy 81

9. The House of God 95

10. Spreading the Word 107

Acknowledgements

Grateful thanks are due to all the cartoonists whose work appears in this book:

Sally Artz, David Austin, Nick Baker, Les Barton, Neil Bennett, Rupert Besley, Rog Bowles,

Hugh Burnett, Ray Chesterton, Clive Collins, Bernard Cookson, Mike Darling,

Roy Davis, Alan de la Nougerede, Stan Eales, Roland Fiddy, Noel Ford, 'Gus',

Tony Holland, 'Holte', Martin Honeysett, Tony Husband, Chic Jacob, Ham Khan,

David Langdon, 'Larry', Ray Lowry, 'MAC', Ed McLachlan, Peter Maddocks,

Johann Mayr [WB], Gerhard Mester, Ged Melling, 'Mike', David Myers, Nick Newman,

Nicola Palombella, Ken Pyne, Viv Quillin, Roy Raymonde, Bryan Reading, Art Reid,

Arnold Roth, Peter Ruge [WB], Albert Rusling, John Ryan, Betty Sack [WB], Alex Talimonov,

Geoff Thompson, Alex Noel Watson, Colin Whittock and Arnold Wiles.

Cartoons by Arnold Roth and 'Mike' appear by kind permission of Punch and

McCrimmon Publishing Co. Ltd, Great Wakering, Essex, respectively.

Cartoons marked 'WB' are by kind permission of Wolfgang Baaske Cartoon Agentur,

Rheinstrasse 22, D—80803 Munich

Preface

If there is a God, I am sure He or She must have a sense of humour. Anyone who can create the duck-billed platypus or the British climate must be kidding sometimes at least, if only a little. And thus I hope that the Most Holy Being in the Universe – who, or whatever that phrase describes – will appreciate in some small measure this modest volume telling the story of Christianity in words and pictures. I also hope that it may help those, of all ages and backgrounds, who wish to learn more about the Church and the Bible but who up to now may have been put off either by the fear of 'God Squad' activists rattling tambourines in their faces or the prospect of ploughing through enormously worthy but desperately lacklustre tomes.

The art of the religious cartoon has itself a venerable history. Though William Hogarth is generally seen as the father of the modern cartoon in all its forms, satirical drawings were much in evidence long before the 18th century and frequently featured prominent members of the Church, whether Catholic or Protestant. Indeed, possibly the first ever political cartoon of any kind was an anonymous 15th-century woodcut depicting the Pope, the Holy Roman Emperor and the kings of France and England. In the early 16th century Pope Alexander VI was shown as a devil and a few years later another drawing had a Jesuit priest with a wolf's head. A particularly striking one from this period was an anti-Protestant woodcut by Erhard Schoen dating from 1521 in which the devil plays a set of bagpipes, using Martin Luther's head as its bellows. And in the 19th century when Charles Darwin put forward his theory of evolution which challenged the biblical version of the Creation and claimed we were all descended from apes, he was mercilessly lampooned as an elderly baboon. The cartoonist's critical pen has also been active in our own times, with issues such as birth control, gay clergy and the ordination of women all inspiring some very trenchant graphic satire. This book, however, is concerned primarily with joke cartoons rather than black humour, and, judging by the fact that some of the drawings included here have already appeared in religious publications such as the *Catholic Herald* and the *Church Times* as well as the more usual humorous journals such as *Private Eye*, *Punch*, *Spectator* and the *Oldie*, it is unlikely that any will cause offence. Quite the opposite, in fact – after nearly 2000 years Christianity is more than mature enough to laugh at itself and see the funny side of ecclesiastical life, and as every clergyman knows, the least effective and most boring sermons are those that lack humour...

I have tried to make the cartoons as varied as cost and copyright availability have allowed and there are drawings by both men and women – even some by a priest – and from countries as varied as Britain, Germany, Italy, New Zealand, Pakistan, Russia and the USA. For invaluable assistance in the preparation of this book I would like to thank the staff of the British Library and the University of London Library at Senate House. Thanks are also due to Bill Neill-Hall of the William Neill-Hall Ltd Literary Agency, whose enthusiasm for the project became infectious after I first proposed it to him at the Frankfurt Book Fair; to my publisher Philip Ralli for taking on the project and making many useful suggestions; and to the designer Mick Keates, the printers, the binders and all at Highland Books for turning the book into such an attractive volume.

Mark Bryant

OLD TESTAMENT TALES

In the Beginning...

According to the first two chapters of the Book of Genesis, God created the Universe in six days and on the seventh rested. In the first five days he created in turn, Heaven, earth, seas, grass, seeds, fruit trees, fish, whales and birds, and on Day 6 made cattle and wild beasts and created man from the dust 'in his own image' and gave him dominion over all the others. This first man was named Adam (which means 'red-skinned') and God planted a garden 'eastward in Eden' in an area bounded by the rivers Tigris and Euphrates and set him up as its gardener, telling him he could eat the fruit of every tree except that of the Tree of Knowledge of Good and Evil – if he did this he would die. He then created a wife for Adam by taking out one of his ribs while he slept and turning it into the first woman, Eve (from the Hebrew for 'life' as she became 'the mother of all living'). One day the snake that lived in the Garden of Eden convinced Eve that they wouldn't die if they ate the fruit from the Tree of Knowledge of Good and Evil but would become like God, so she ate some of the fruit and gave some to Adam to eat. Immediately they realized they were naked and God was so angry that he expelled them from the Garden placing angels and 'a flaming sword which turned every way' at the gate to prevent their re-entry. In addition he personally punished Eve, by making her give birth only in pain (their children were Cain, Abel and Seth), and condemned Adam to live by toiling the earth until he died – at the age of 930.

'I can't even get him to put up a set of shelves.'

'I really <u>was</u> made in your image!'

God drowned everyone else – in a warm, caring sort of way of course

Noah and The Flood. According to Genesis Chapter VI, Noah was the eldest son of Lamech and was born when his father was 182. Lamech was himself the son of history's oldest man, Methuselah (who died aged 969) and was a descendant of Adam's third son Seth. When Noah was aged about 600, God confided in him that he was fed up with mankind's wickedness and would drown all living things except Noah, his wife, his three sons (Japheth, Shem and Ham) and their wives, and one pair (male and female) of each variety of living creature (plus seven pairs of 'clean' animals and birds – such as cattle, sheep and chickens but not camels, pigs, or birds of prey). He then commanded Noah to build out of gopher wood (cypress) a large, three-storey ark (a chest-shaped container), 450 feet long, which would float on the waters. A week after Noah had finished the boat and all were aboard it rained for 40 days and 40 nights and the whole world was flooded. 150 days later the waters began to subside and they found themselves on Mt Ararat (Armenia). To see if it was safe to disembark, Noah sent out first a raven (which never returned) then, a week later, a dove which brought back an olive branch. When a further week later he sent out the dove again and it didn't return he knew that it had reached dry land and they unloaded the ark. Noah killed some of the animals and birds as the first ever biblical burnt offering and God created the rainbow as a sign of this new covenant with mankind. Noah himself lived a further 350 years and died aged 950.

Sodom and Gomorah. A direct descendant of Noah's second son, Shem, was Abraham, the founder of the Israelite nation. A divine command instructed him to take his family and his nephew Lot to a promised land which was later revealed to be Canaan (Palestine) – from the Hebrew for 'lowland' – on the River Jordan. After arriving, he was told he would have numerous progeny (his name means 'father of a multitude' in Hebrew) and would prosper. This quickly became the case and as the land couldn't support both his and Lot's flocks and herdsmen he gave his nephew the choice of habitat and Lot chose the fertile plain (the Jordan valley) in which already lay five cities – Sodom, Gomorrah, Admah, Zeboim and Zoar –

under the rule of King Chedorlaomer of Elam (a kingdom adjoining Babylonia). Abraham, meanwhile, stayed in the hills. Later the cities rebelled unsuccessfully against Elam rule and their inhabitants were scattered or captured. Amongst the prisoners was Lot and when Abraham heard of this he took 318 men and rescued him. Sodom and Gomorah then gained a reputation for vice and homosexuality and God sent two angels to Lot to warn him that they were soon to be destroyed. Lot fled from Sodom to the mountains above Zoar but his wife disobeyed God's injunction not to look back and, as she gazed at the fire and brimstone which destroyed all the cities of the plain, she became a pillar of salt.

*'Still, you managed to get her into
sheltered accommodation, Lot.'*

Joseph and His Many-Coloured Coat.
Joseph was the 11th of the 12 sons of
Jacob, Abraham's grandson. He was born
in Padan-Aram (Mesopotamia) and was
his father's favourite which led to much
jealousy amongst his brothers. He was also
a great dreamer and his mother Rachel
made him a coat of many colours like
those shown on Egyptian monuments.
One day his jealous brothers sold him to
some passing Arabs, covered his coat with
goats' blood and gave it to Jacob saying
that he had been killed. The Arabs next
went to Egypt and sold Joseph as a slave
to Potiphar, captain of the royal guard to
the Pharaoh (probably Apepi II), but
Potiphar soon released him and gave him
control of his household until he was
jailed when falsely accused of trying to rape
Potiphar's wife. In prison, he demonstrated
his skill at dream-interpretation to
another inmate, Pharaoh's butler. When
the butler was released he recommended
Joseph as someone who could interpret a
persistent dream of Pharaoh's. This
dream featured seven lean cows
eating seven fat ones and seven
bad ears of corn eating seven
good ones. He correctly
deduced that they
symbolized seven years of
plenty followed by seven
of famine and was given
extremely high rank.
When later, during the
time of famine, his
brothers come to Egypt to
buy grain (which Joseph

> **The 12 Tribes of Israel**
> *Joseph and his eleven brothers – Reuben,
> Simeon, Levi, Judah, Dan, Naphtali, Gad,
> Asher, Issacar, Zebulun and Benjamin –
> were the founders of the 12 Tribes of Israel.
> Their father, Jacob, had been given the new
> name of Israel – fighter or soldier of God –
> after he had wrestled with a man who
> turned out to be God: 'Thy name shall be
> called no more Jacob, but Israel, for thou
> hast striven with God and with men, and
> hast prevailed' (Genesis Chapter XXXII)*

had wisely stored in the years of plenty)
they didn't recognize him as he was now
so powerful. However, he later revealed
himself to them and forgave them for
their earlier wickedness.

*'... or was it seven fat cows ate seven ... No, there were
some cows, er... seven thin ones ... I think... That's it!
Seven ... er... hang about ...'*

*'Old bedsteads, wheels, mattresses ... it's disgusting –
and now what have we got in the bulrushes ... ?'*

Moses in the Bulrushes. In Joseph's time the Israelites prospered in Egypt but when a new Pharaoh came to the throne (probably Rameses II), he became alarmed at their power and fast-increasing population and made them into slaves, issuing also an edict that all male children born to them should be drowned in the Nile in an attempt to limit their numbers. It was at this time (*c.*1571 BC) that Moses was born, the third child (he had an older brother Aaron and a sister Miriam) of Amram, grandson of Levi (one of Joseph's brothers and Jacob's third son). However, his mother Jochebed disobeyed the edict and hid him in a box-shaped boat or ark made of reeds amongst the bulrushes on the Nile's bank, telling her daughter Miriam to stand guard over him. One day, Pharaoh's daughter spotted the baby and took him into the royal household, Miriam suggested a local woman as a wet nurse (in fact Jochebed), and the child was given the Egyptian name Moses, from the Hebrew *mosheh* meaning 'drawn out from the water'.

The Plagues of Egypt. Moses became very well educated but one day, seeing an Egyptian mistreating an Israelite, he killed the Egyptian and hid him in the sand. When this became known he fled Egypt for Midian in the Sinai peninsula, later marrying one of the daughters of the local priest, Jethro. It was in Midian that he also saw a burning bush and through the flames Jehovah commanded him to return to Egypt and free the Israelites from their bondage. After the death of Pharaoh he then returned and negotiated with the obstinate new ruler who only agreed after Moses had inflicted on them ten plagues: i) turning the Nile into blood; then ii) plagues of frogs; iii) lice; iv) flies; v) sick cattle; vi) boils; vii) huge hailstones; viii) locusts; ix) darkness; x) the death of the Egyptians' first-born children. Pharaoh then let them go and they took with them much of the Egyptians' silver, gold, jewellery and clothing as they headed back to Sinai.

'A plague of frogs in the north will move slowly south, replaced over the weekend by a plague of locusts. The outlook for...'

The Parting of the Red Sea. Exodus Chapter XIV tells of the Israelites' escape from Egypt (where they had been held in captivity for 430 years). In all, 600,000 men together with their dependants and cattle fled towards Canaan (Palestine), being guided by a pillar of cloud in daylight and a pillar of fire at night. They were pursued by a huge Egyptian army of cavalry and infantry – including 600 hand-picked charioteers – which caught up with them on what is now generally believed to be a point on the Gulf of Suez, the most north-westerly prolongation of the Red Sea. Here their leader, Moses, raised his rod and performed a miracle: 'And Moses stretched out his hand over the sea, and the Lord caused the sea to go back by a strong east wind all that night, and made the sea dry land, and the waters were divided' (XIV, 21). Once the Israelites were safely across, Moses held out his hand again, the waters closed and the pursuing Egyptian forces were all drowned.

The 10 Commandments and the Ark of the Covenant. When, three months later, the Israelites reached the Sinai peninsula in the most easterly part of Egypt, Moses went up into the mountains and fasted for 40 days and 40 nights (as later would the prophet Elijah and Jesus when they went into the wilderness). After this period, God gave him two stone tablets on which were written, in a divine hand, the 10 Commandments. However, on his return he was so outraged that the Israelites had taken to worshipping a golden calf (made by Moses's brother Aaron) that he broke the stones and had to go up in the mountains again where, after a similar period of fasting, he received two more. For these he made a special portable chest or ark out of acacia wood inlaid with gold and carried on two poles. This, the Ark of the Covenant (measuring *c*.3.75 x 2.25 x 2.25ft) was carried by the Israelites thoughout their wanderings in the wilderness (40 years in all), and later also held the Book of the Law which Moses wrote, a golden pot containing some of the manna which had saved them from starvation in the desert, and the special rod with which Moses and Aaron had worked miracles. Eventually the Israelites came to the promised land of Canaan (Palestine) but Moses never reached it. He died aged 120 after seeing the plain from Mount Nebo (Jebel Neba).

'There's been a slight accident – can you spare ten more..?'

The Fall of Jericho. The Israelites' leader, Moses, had in fact died after seeing the important Philistine stronghold of Jericho 'the city of palm trees' which lay on the west bank of the River Jordan, and blocked the advance of his people into Palestine when they came out of the wilderness four decades after leaving Egypt. In Chapter I of the Book of Joshua we learn how Moses's successor, Joshua, sent out spies into the city to find its weak points and then commanded 40,000 of his warriors, headed by seven priests blowing seven trumpets made of rams' horns, to circle the walls once a day for a week, carrying the Ark of the Covenant. On the seventh day, when the priests' trumpets sounded he ordered all his people to shout, 'and it came to pass, when the people heard the sound of the trumpet, and the people shouted with a great shout, that the wall fell down flat, so that the people went up unto the city, every man straight before him, and they took the city' (VI, 21). The fall of Jericho is now generally held to have taken place in about 1451 BC.

> **The Philistines**
> The Philistines were a powerful race of Phoenician descent who occupied an area known as Philistia – Palestina is a Greek rendering of 'land of the Philistines' – which stretched from Jaffa to the Egyptian desert south of Gaza and which included the land God had granted to his chosen people, the Israelites. Moses had deliberately skirted around their domain in the south in order to reach the Jordan valley.

Samson and Delilah. After the death of Joshua, the Israelites were frequently conquered by other tribes in the area of Palestine, but at intervals revolutionary leaders called 'judges' managed to throw off the yoke of the oppressors and ruled in their stead. One of the most noteworthy of these was Samson. Of the tribe of Dan, he fought against the Philistines who had been the dominant power in Palestine for 40 years. He was brought up as a Nazirite (as was John the Baptist) – a sect which forbade the drinking of alcohol and the cutting of hair or beards. Hence his name, which comes from the Hebrew *shimson* or sun-like, as his long hair was like the rays of the sun. Outlawed for burning crops and killing 1000 men with the jawbone of an ass, he met a Philistine woman, Delilah, who, bribed by her rulers, tricked him into revealing that his strength lay in his hair. She then cut it off, and he was captured, blinded and imprisoned in the great Philistine city of Gaza. Some time later, the Philistines decided to display him for sport at the great festival to their main deity, Dagon the fish-god. However, his hair had by then grown back and, his strength returned, Samson, who'd been tied to the two pillars supporting the roof, pulled down the temple, killing himself and 3000 worshippers. He had ruled as a judge for 20 years.

'We've made a big mistake here, chief. Samson's twice as bad since we turned him into a skinhead!'

'To be absolutely honest, we were rather expecting Goliath to win.'

The Slaying of Goliath. During the reign of King Saul, the first king of the Israelites, a giant called Goliath from the important Philistine city of Gath, contemptuously challenged anyone from the Israelite army to fight him in single combat. The challenge was taken up by Saul's armour-bearer, a young shepherd, poet and harpist called David, who was the youngest of eight sons of Jesse from Bethlehem and had been anointed by the prophet/judge Samuel as a future king of Israel. Though much smaller than Goliath, who was armed with a spear and sword and wore a brass helmet and body armour, David toppled him with a single stone slingshot to the forehead, then killed him with the giant's own sword and cut off his head. David was later elected king of the tribe of Judah and then, at the age of 30, of all the 12 tribes of Israel. He set up his capital in Jerusalem, the 'City of David' and inaugurated the building of the Great Temple to house the Ark of the Covenant (completed by his son Solomon). He wrote 73 of the 150 Psalms and after reigning for 40 years died aged 71 in c.1015 BC.

Jonah and the Whale. The Hebrew prophet Jonah was born in Gath-hepher, a village near Nazareth, Palestine, in the 9th century BC. He correctly predicted the restoration of Israelite power in the area under their warrior King Jeroboam II c.822 BC but is best known for his holy mission to the great Assyrian capital of Nineveh, which then had a population of about 120,000. Told by God to 'go...and cry against it; for their wickedness is come before me', he ignored the command and tried to flee from the Lord's domain, embarking at Joppa (modern Jaffa) for Tarshish (a Phoenician town in southern Spain). However, a storm blew up in the Mediterranean and all aboard except Jonah (who was asleep) called on their gods to rescue them. When this didn't work they woke Jonah, drew lots to see whose god had caused the storm and when the lot fell on him he confessed he had disobeyed the Lord. He then suggested that they should throw him into the sea to appease the Lord. This they did, the storm subsided and Jonah was swallowed by a 'great fish'. Inside the whale, Jonah prayed for forgiveness and after three days and nights he was vomited out onto dry land. This time when ordered to Nineveh, he went, and declared to the citizens that they would all be destroyed in 40 days if they didn't mend their ways and repent of their sins. In great fear, the people, even the Assyrian king and the aristocracy, fasted, prayed and wore sackcloth and ashes and were thus saved.

'He never forgave the whale...'

HEAVEN AND HELL

God in Heaven

Heaven is where God resides (seated on a throne), together with Jesus (on his right hand), the Holy Spirit (or Ghost), the angels, and the souls of all the righteous people who once lived on earth. The word 'heaven' itself comes from an Old English word, the Hebrew word being *shamayim*, which refers to seven 'heavens', in only the seventh of which resides God (Islam also holds this view). Paradise (a Persian word meaning a nobleman's park or garden – cf Garden of Eden) was seen as the third Heaven in which the righteous dead would dwell until the Last Judgement when they would join God in the highest Heaven. Originally, Heaven was thought of as being a place of eternal light above the clouds and the stars of the firmament (the apparent vaulting arch or dome which, to the ancients, seemed to cover the earth and, unlike the terrestial world, seemed to be permanent and unchanging), the visible sky being its floor. The other half of the universe consisted entirely of the earth (the earth was then seen as

'I don't suppose it matters much, but I always understood that you were seated on His right.'

flat). Later views had the earth at the centre of the universe with everything revolving around it and the Heavens as various outer spheres like onion skins beyond the inner spheres containing the sun and moon, planets, stars etc. However, with the advances in modern scientific knowledge of the universe these ideas have changed somewhat and 'heaven' is now open to various interpretations, including a state a bliss which has no particular location in physical terms.

'There have been some changes around here…'

Souls, Spirits and Ghosts. What Christians see as being worthy or sinful and thus eligible at resurrection for entry to Heaven or Hell is not the physical body, which decays after death, but rather a supposedly immortal 'inner light' – the principle of life as well as thought, action, emotion etc. – which is able to separate from the body at death. The Old English word 'soul' and the Latin-derived 'spirit' (which also means 'a breath of air') both refer to this individual life-force. And when on rare occasions a soul/spirit appears to a still-living human being (perhaps while it is still in Purgatory as some would hold) it is described as a ghost.

This belief in an immortal element in man has a long history, as has discussion over its exact location. The Ancient Greeks placed it in the heart (viewing the brain as a sort of radiator to cool the circulation), the Jews put it in the blood (hence the strict *kosher* practice of drawing off blood from meat to be consumed). Modern science focuses on the brain as the centre of thought, feeling and morality – or 'mind' – but other candidates in history and in various religions have included the bowels, liver and kidneys amongst others. Good souls which have reached Heaven are usually depicted as angels dressed in white gowns with white wings and playing harps.

*'The new ones are always the same,
until they get used to the novelty.'*

The Holy Spirit (also called the Holy
Ghost) – by whom Jesus was conceived
and with whom Jesus baptized his
converts – has been the subject of much
controversy in the Christian Church over
the centuries, but one view is that he is a
kind of divine energy.

a relation to God, e.g. Gabriel means 'man of God').

Of these, the highest, Michael, is leader of the armies of Heaven and is mentioned in the Books of Daniel, Jude and Revelation. Gabriel is named as the messenger to Daniel, John the Baptist's father and Jesus's mother. In the 12th century the cherubim were depicted as child-angels (cherubs or *putti* from the Italian for 'boy') and in the late Renaissance female angels were introduced. There are apparently countless numbers of angels and in the Middle Ages there was much speculation as to their nature. One ecclesiastical scholar, John Duns Scotus, from Scotland became renowned for his hair-splitting pedantry – such as trying to figure out how many angels would fit on a pin-head – giving rise to the modern word 'dunce'.

The Orders of Angels. The Greek word *aggelos* means a messenger and the angels were originally seen as messengers from God. In Christianity they are celestial beings – of a higher order than man but otherwise not dissimilar to him in appearance though made of pure spirit – who reside with God in Heaven. They first appear in Genesis when one is stated as guarding the entrance to Eden after Adam and Eve have been expelled (in earlier Ancient Egyptian and Assyrian society, winged beasts were depicted as guarding royal palaces). The nine divisions (or choirs) of angels popularized in the 5th century and arranged in three triads are (in descending order): Archangels, Angels and Principalities; Dominions, Virtues and Powers; Seraphim, Cherubim and Thrones. The seven archangels are Michael, Gabriel, Raphael, Uriel, Chamuel, Jophiel and Zadkiel (the suffix 'el' in Hebrew implies

'Aussie?'

20

Purgatory. According to Roman Catholic tradition, Purgatory is a place – neither Heaven nor Hell – or state of suffering after death in which the souls of the dead are purged of any remaining sin by various punishments including torture by fire until they are fit to enter Heaven. Their progress there can be aided by the still living by the holding of masses, the act of prayer and the giving of alms (donations of money to the Church). The Protestant faith totally rejects the doctrine and holds that after death people's souls go straight to glory in Heaven or eternal damnation in Hell. (A number of other religions have a similar concept of Purgatory.)

'No mate – this is Purgatory. That's Eternity over there.'

Hell, Perdition and Limbo. Hell is where all the sinful souls denied access to the joys of Heaven go (perdition, from the Latin *perdo*, is the state of being lost). Medieval ecclesiastical scholars also claimed that on the outskirts of Hell was an area known as Limbo (from the word for 'a border') whose inhabitants were unbaptized children and those good souls who unfortunately died before the coming of Jesus. Hell proper, though, is the place of eternal suffering. Some imagery derives from the Hades of the Ancient Greeks, the underground (hence Inferno, from the word meaning 'lower') abode of departed spirits who had failed to reach the happy fields of the celestial Elysium – its lowest depths were known as Tartarus. Hell is also known as Gehenna in the Bible, referring to the Valley of Hinnom (Hebrew Ge-Hinnom) near Jerusalem where child sacrifices were made. The damned in Hell are traditionally portrayed as being naked (without wings or harps) and immersed in boiling oil or consumed by fire and brimstone (sulphur) whilst being tormented by semi-human, goat-like demons with pointed tails and wielding tridents.

'Another bloody Prozac overdose!'

'This is absurd! We shall be done under the Trade Descriptions Act!'

The Visions of the Apocalypse. The Book of John, also known as The Apocalypse ('uncovering') or Revelations tells of a number of mystical experiences reported by the saint. After the introductory sections we are given a picture of Heaven, with God surrounded by 24 elders, seven angels and a slain Lamb (representing Jesus) which opened a scroll closed with seven seals. Each time the Lamb broke one of the first four seals a figure appeared, mounted on a horse. The first (on a white horse) had a bow, wore a crown and 'went forth conquering'; the second (on a red horse) had a sword and had 'power... to take peace from the earth'; the third (on a black horse) held a pair of balances, and the fourth rider (on a pale horse) was Death. The fifth seal revealed those who had been martyred for their faith, and the breaking of the sixth caused the sun to blacken and produced a huge earthquake. The 144,000 members of God's chosen people were then identified prior to the opening of the seventh seal after which seven angels sounded in turn seven trumpets and emptied seven phials of God's wrath onto the world, destroying everything in various horrific ways until all evil was finally vanquished at Armageddon. This was a real place (Hebrew Har Megiddo, 'mount of Megiddo') near Jezreel, Palestine, on whose plain Pharaoh Thotmes III of Egypt had defeated the Canaanites and later (after the arrival of the Israelites) Pharaoh Necho had killed the Israelite King Josiah – both battles having been extremely bloody. Finally, on Doomsday or the Day of Judgement, John's dream showed all being judged according to their deeds and either cast into Hell or saved. He then saw a vision of a new Heaven and a new earth and out of the new Heaven he saw a new Jerusalem coming down to earth.

25

Satan, Lucifer, Beelzebub and Mephistopheles. Satan was not always evil. His name in Hebrew means simply 'adversary' and he became the opponent of God, Jesus and all Christendom, but originally he was an angel. According to Jude there was a revolt in Heaven and Satan (whose sin we are told in Timothy was pride) and his followers were ejected and sent to earth to lead the Chosen People into the temptation of breaking the 10 Commandments and committing sins. These, then, were the so-called 'fallen angels'. The name 'the Devil' comes from the Greek for 'a slanderer' and is also applied to Satan. His actual angelic name was Lucifer ('light-bearer'). Beelzebub (originally Baal-zebub, 'lord of the flies') was the name of the Philistine fly-god of the city of Ekron in Palestine at the time of the Israelites' arrival. Satan's followers were also known as 'demons', though this Greek-derived word originally meant any spirit, whether good or bad. One of these wicked angels, identified as Mephistopheles, is seen bargaining for a human's soul in the story of Dr Faustus popularized by Marlowe and Goethe.

'Quentin ... we've got nice!'

THE LIFE
OF JESUS

The Birth of Jesus

A ccording to the Gospel of Luke and others in the New Testament, during the reign of the first Roman Emperor, Augustus Caesar, the high-ranking angel Gabriel (who had previously appeared to Daniel in the Old Testament) came to Roman-occupied Palestine – then ruled by the Jewish King Herod – and announced to a Jewish priest Zacharias, while he was burning incense in the Temple in Jerusalem, that he and his wife Elizabeth – both descendants of Aaron and thereby of the tribe of Levi (Jacob's third son) – would have a child (John the Baptist) who would be the forerunner of God's son when he shortly appeared on earth in human form. Soon afterwards, the angel appeared to Elizabeth's cousin Miriam (in Greek Maria or Mary) who lived in Nazareth in the northerly province of Galilee. She was herself of the tribe of Judah (Jacob's fourth son) and, though she was then a virgin and already engaged to a carpenter from Nazareth called Joseph, the angel told her she would give birth to God's son, the Messiah ('anointed one'), whose coming had been prophesied in the Old Testament. Joseph, at first suspicious, soon became convinced of this and married Mary.

Then, when Mary was heavily pregnant, both travelled to Bethlehem near Jerusalem in the province of Judaea some 70 miles to the south because the Romans had ordered a census of the inhabitants of Palestine and everyone had to return to their town of origin and register their names (Joseph was a descendant of the Jewish King David of

'He believed everything – the Angel, the Virgin Birth – the lot –!!'

Bethlehem). However, on arrival they found the place overcrowded with others come to register and, finding no accommodation, had to stay in a stable where Mary gave birth to a boy, subsequently named Joshua (Latinized as Jesus) and, lacking a cradle, the baby slept in one of the mangers that held the animals' food. Some shepherds in the hills above Bethlehem that night saw a vision of angels proclaiming the birth of the Saviour of Mankind and came down to pay their respects. The day of Jesus's birth (Christmas Day) was later fixed as 25 December to coincide with the date of the winter solstice on the Julian Calendar and the Roman festival of Saturnalia and it is now held to have been six to eight years earlier than given.

'Your horoscope for 24th December says you will experience a miracle.'

The Three Wise Men. On the eighth day after his birth, Jesus was circumcised according to Jewish practice and, following the formal 40 days of ceremonial purification, was officially presented at the Temple in Jerusalem. Mary and Joseph then took him back to Bethlehem where he was visited by three wise men known as Magi (a priestly order) from Parthia (Persia, modern Iran), who had seen an unrecorded star in their country, associated it with the birth of a great king, and tracked it until they found it shining above Jesus's birthplace. On arrival they presented the baby with gifts of gold, frankincense and myrrh (the latter two being ingredients of the oil which Jewish priests used for holy anointments). However, King Herod learnt of the visit and, fearing that if this was indeed the long-promised Messiah who would found a kingdom that would never pass away and thus would almost certainly take his crown or that of his descendants, asked the Magi to give him details of the baby's whereabouts, pretending that he wanted to worship him too. The Magi, though, were warned in a dream not to tell and departed.

Jesus and the Temple

By the time Jesus was 12, Herod had died and Mary and Joseph had returned to Nazareth in Galilee. For the first time, that year they decided to take Jesus along with them on their annual pilgrimage south to Jerusalem and the Great Temple. (The Jews only had one temple, an enormous edifice to God in Jerusalem which had been built originally by King David and his son Solomon to house the Ark of the Covenant.) After they arrived they were amazed when the child seemed able to discuss fine points of theology with the priests. They later returned to Nazareth and for the next 18 years Jesus worked at his father's profession of a carpenter. Later, when he had begun his peripatetic ministry, he came to Jerusalem again, this time seated on an ass (the large white cross on a donkey's back is a symbol of this) and the people threw clothes and leaves in his path in his honour. He then went up to the Temple 'and cast out all them that sold and bought...and overthrew the tables of the money-changers, and the seats of them that sold doves. And said unto them: "It is written, My house shall be called the house of prayer; but ye have made it a den of thieves" ' (Matthew Chapter XXI, 12–13).

Thwarted, Herod then decreed that every child under two in Bethlehem and its suburbs should be killed in an effort to destroy Jesus. Joseph was warned of the coming slaughter in a dream and he and his family escaped southwards to the valley of the Nile in Egypt before the killing started. They didn't return to Palestine until after Herod's death.

'I don't mind the wise men and the shepherds – it's the medical students I object to.'

John the Baptist. John the Baptist's coming had been predicted by the prophets Isaiah and Malachi. He was born during the reign of Emperor Augustus in Juttah, a hill-village in Judaea, about six months before the birth of Jesus. He came of a priestly family, his father being a direct descendant of Moses's brother Aaron, and his mother Elizabeth was a cousin of Jesus's mother Mary. He was brought up as a Nazirite, like Samson, and neither cut his hair nor drank alcohol. In about AD 29 he began preaching in the wilderness to great crowds and washing away the sins of the repentant in the River Jordan. This 'baptism' (from the Greek word 'to dip') earned him the name John the Baptist. However, he said that soon one would come who would baptize with the Holy Spirit. This would be Jesus, who was in fact baptized himself by John prior to spending 40 days in the wilderness being tempted by the Devil. John's life, however, was short-lived. Having publicly condemned the tetrarch of Galilee (Herod Antipas, son of Herod the Great), for living with his half-brother's wife Herodias, he was imprisoned in the fort of Macharaeus, 3800 feet above the Dead Sea. While there he sent two of his disciples (Andrew and his brother Peter, later Jesus's disciples) to ask if Jesus was indeed the promised Messiah. They returned with convincing evidence but meanwhile, at a banquet, the erotic dancing of Herodias's daughter Salome had so pleased Herod that he granted her any wish. As the Baptist had criticized Herodias's relationship with the tetrarch, she told Salome to ask for John's head on a plate and he was duly executed.

JOHN THE
BAPTIST
BALLOONS

'They were quite meek until they inherited the earth.'

The Sermon on the Mount. When Jesus heard of John the Baptist's imprisonment, he left Judaea and went to Galilee where John had been incarcerated and began preaching and healing the sick. Walking around the Sea of Galilee (the 12¾-mile-long freshwater Lake of Gennesaret) he then invited four fishermen – Andrew and Peter (already disciples of John the Baptist) and James and John – to be his disciples, saying he would make them into 'fishers of men'. He later went up into the mountains and began to preach to huge crowds the famous Sermon on the Mount in which he blessed the peacemakers, the meek, the poor in spirit and others, and detailed the wording of the Lord's Prayer.

Feeding the 5000. When the news of John the Baptist's execution reached Jesus, he immediately headed out to the desert again. Thousands followed him and when night fell his disciples wanted to send the crowd away as they had no food to give them except the five loaves and two fish that they themselves had brought. Jesus, however, had other plans. 'And he commanded the multitude to sit down on the grass, and took the five loaves, and the two fishes and, looking up to Heaven, he blessed, and brake, and gave the loaves to his disciples, and the disciples to the multitude. And they did all eat, and were filled: and they took up the fragments that remained twelve baskets full. And they that had eaten were about five thousand, beside women and children' (Matthew Chapter XIV, 19–21). He then sent them all away.

Walking on Water. After feeding the 5000 who came with him into the desert following the execution of John the Baptist, Jesus climbed up a mountain and prayed, having sent his disciples on ahead in a boat across the Sea of Galilee. However, the sea became stormy and 'in the fourth watch of the night Jesus went unto them, walking on the sea' (Matthew Chapter XIV, 25). This frightened them and they thought he was a ghost. But Jesus reassured them and asked Peter to get out of the boat and walk towards him across the water. This he did for a short distance then became afraid of the winds and sank. Jesus lifted him out of the water, said 'O thou of little faith, wherefore didst thou doubt?' and helped him into the boat. Immediately, the storm subsided.

Raising Lazarus from the Dead. Jesus had performed a number of miracles – feeding the 5000, walking on water, turning water into wine etc. – but one of the most spectacular was making Lazarus come back to life after he had been dead for four days. Lazarus and his sisters Martha and Mary were good friends of Jesus. They lived in Bethany, a village on the Mount of Olives about two miles from Jerusalem, and Jesus often meditated in this area and would stay at their house. However, when Lazarus contracted a terminal illness, Jesus didn't come at first to heal him as he had done for so many others, but instead – for greater effect – decided to allow him to die. Then, after he had been buried in a sepulchre consisting of a cave whose entrance had been blocked up with a boulder (the usual kind of interment in those times), Jesus arrived in Bethany, went straight up to the grave, had the rock removed and, in front of a crowd of mourners, commanded: 'Lazarus, come forth.' To the assembly's amazement, Lazarus then walked out, still dressed in his shroud. This story is told in the Gospel of John Chapter XI, which also contains the Bible's shortest verse (v.35): 'Jesus wept.'

'Sorry, he doesn't do toasters.'

The Parable of the Good Samaritan.

A parable (from the Greek *parabole* meaning a comparison) is a 'fictitious narrative used to typify moral or spiritual relations' (*OED*) – in effect it is a veiled form of speech in which instruction or reproof is conveyed indirectly by giving a similar example. There are a number of parables in the Old Testament, and in the New Testament Jesus tells a total of 36. Notable amongst these are those of the Sower, the Lost Sheep, the Talents and the Prodigal Son. The parable of the Good Samaritan occurs in Luke Chapter X and is told in answer to a question by a lawyer about what he must do to inherit eternal life. Amongst the conditions cited are loving your neighbour as yourself, but then the lawyer asks: 'And who is my neighbour?' In reply Jesus tells a story about a man travelling from Jerusalem to Jericho who is attacked by thieves who strip him, beat him up and leave him for dead. A priest saw him but passed by, as did a Levite – one of the sacred Jewish castes that officiated at the Temple in Jerusalem – but a Samaritan saw him and dressed his wounds, took him to an inn and gave the innkeeper money to look after him. At this time the Jews had a great prejudice against the Samaritans who also lived in Palestine and held similar religious views to them. The Samaritan's action was thus an important lesson for the lawyer. Jesus asked him: 'Which now of these three ... was neighbour unto him that fell among the thieves?' and the lawyer responded 'He that shewed mercy on him.' Then Jesus said 'Go, and do thou likewise.'

The Last Supper. In the last year of his life, Jesus and his 12 disciples were outside Jerusalem during the feast of Passover, which celebrated the Israelites' escape from the tenth and worst plague in Egypt – the angel of death which killed the first-born in every family having quite literally 'passed over' their houses which they had identified by marking them with the blood of animals. The feast itself was celebrated by the drinking of wine and the eating of unleavened bread (bread made without yeast) and took place each year in March. Knowing that this would be his 'last supper' Jesus had decided to make the Passover feast have a new significance. He sent Peter and John into Jerusalem to find an upstairs room in a house they could use and in the evening they all assembled there. Jesus then drank some wine and ate some bread and declared that it would be the last time he would do so. He then passed the bread around saying 'This is my body which is given for you' and then the wine saying 'This is my blood of the new testament which is shed for you' and asked them to repeat this ceremony in his memory when he was gone. He then said that one of the company would soon betray him and they all went out to the nearby Mount of Olives, where he often went, and while Jesus prayed in an olive grove called the Garden of Gethsemane (*gethesemane* means 'oil press') on the hillside, the others slept until Judas appeared with a large crowd including priests and elders and went up to Jesus and kissed him, thus identifying him and leading to his arrest. Peter cut off one of the officers' ears with his sword but Jesus told him not to resist and all the disciples fled.

'Tonight, one of you will betray me'

36

The Crucifixion. After Jesus had been led away, he was taken to the house of Caiaphas the high priest of Jerusalem who accused him of blasphemy in claiming he was the son of God, for which the penalty was death. The following day, a Friday (subsequently called Good Friday), they then took him to the Roman Governor, Pontius Pilate, who was procurator of Judaea and normally resident in Caesarea but was in Jerusalem for the huge annual Passover festival in case there were any riots. Pilate then, discovering that Jesus was from Galilee, thought to send him to be judged by Herod, the tetrarch of that province, but Herod deferred to him. As it was customary for the Romans to release one Jewish prisoner at the Passover festival he then asked the crowd which of the two most celebrated captives – Jesus or Barabbas, a rebel and murderer – should be set free. The crowd, egged on by the priests, cried for Barabbas to be released and for Jesus to be crucified (a common death-sentence at that time, involving tying or nailing the victim to a wooden cross until they expired). Pilate, knowing that Jesus was innocent, then theatrically washed his hands in a basin before the crowd and said 'I am innocent of the blood of this just person, see ye to it' and the crowd responded: 'His blood be on us, and on our children.' The Roman guards then whipped him (commonly done before a crucifixion), dressed him in a purple robe (the dress of a Roman emperor), put a crown of thorns on his head, a reed in his hand as a sceptre and mockingly bowed before him crying 'Hail, King of the Jews' (Jesus had said that he was king but that his kingdom was not on earth). He was then led away to Calvary (Latin for the Aramaic *golgotha*, place of skulls), the main execution site to the north of the city. Jesus carried the cross some of the way but found it too heavy, so a North African, Simon the Cyrenian, was forced to

BARABBAS VERDICT RULED UNSAFE

carry it. He was crucified with two robbers at 9am, and by 3pm the same day had died. (A soldier later struck him in the left side of his chest with a spear to make sure he was dead.) At the moment of his death there was a great earthquake and the veil which hid the Holy of Holies in the Temple was torn in two, thus signifying that anyone can worship without the intervention of a priest.

The Resurrection

Jesus had always said that three days after his death he would rise from the grave and so a Roman guard was placed outside to make sure that his disciples didn't steal the body and pretend it had risen. The grave itself was not a common criminal's tomb (as would normally be the case for one who had been publicly executed) but a rich man's one. This was because one of the Jewish council which had condemned him (Joseph of Aramathea) had asked for his body and another, Nicodemus, had supplied myrrh and aloes to embalm him (both had secretly supported him). On the Sunday (now celebrated as Easter Sunday), various followers went to the grave to anoint Jesus's body but found that the rock had been removed, the grave was empty and two young men dressed in white told them that he had risen from the dead (the guards had already gone). Jesus himself then appeared to some of the disciples in various parts of Jerusalem and later was even seen by Peter, John and others while they were fishing at night miles away in Galilee. Jesus was then seen by the disciples fairly regularly for 40 days after his death until, accompanied by them, he went to Bethany (where his friend Lazarus has been raised from the dead) and literally ascended into Heaven, disappearing into a cloud, this day being marked thereafter as Ascension Day.

SAINTS AND SINNERS

What is a Saint?

The modern sense of the word 'saint' (Latin *sanctus* from the word for consecration or making sacred) to mean a deceased holy person canonized (i.e. officially recognized) by the Christian Church has only really existed since the 6th century. Prior to that the word was applied in the Old Testament to any one of the Israelites or Chosen People, and in the New Testament it referred to any member of the Christian community. It was first used in the way most common today when referring to those who were martyred for their Christian faith, and later to the so-called 'confessors' who admitted their faith but weren't actually martyred as a result. In the early years, it was only necessary for a local bishop to declare someone a saint but nowadays, in the Roman Catholic Church at least, only the Pope can do so. Catholicism also allows for a lower grade of sanctity known as 'beatification' in which a person can be declared blessed (i.e. favoured of God) but this only carries

restricted authorization to be venerated. Relics (bones, clothing etc.), and in the Eastern Orthodox Church images of the saints, known as icons, are also given due reverence. (However, the Anglican and other churches of the Reformation movement, while allowing the honouring of saints, do not permit their veneration.) These images of saints depict them dressed in their professional clothes (armour for soldiers, vestments for priests etc.) and all have a halo (the disc of the sun), nimbus (Latin for cloud) or aureole (gold disc) around their heads, sometimes emanating rays like those of the sun or stars (this motif originated in pre-Christian times in images of the divine Roman Emperors). Martyrs are additionally shown with the crown of eternal life, the palm of triumph and a symbol of some kind, usually the instrument of their martyrdom (e.g. St Catherine's wheel). Images of non-martyred saints are normally shown with the object representing their particular virtue (e.g. St Dominic's sparrow). Jesus's Apostles are all called saints (except for Judas Iscariot), as are his parents Mary and Joseph, some of the angels (e.g. St Michael), and the (non-Apostolic) Gospel writers Luke and Mark. In addition, all the popes from St Peter until the end of the 4th century were called saints, as were a number of kings and queens including Edward the Confessor of England, Olaf II of Norway, Louis IX of France and Stephen I of Hungary.

EDWARD THE HELPFUL

'Lust is top of the charts, closely followed by Adultery with Anger slipping to third place ...'

The Seven Deadly Sins. A sinner is someone who transgresses divine law or a principle of morality. Sins can be of omission – where one neglects to do what the law of God commands – or of commission, involving doing what the law forbids. Some hold the doctrine of original sin, i.e. that we are born with an innate propensity to do evil, but others contend that if you are unaware of the law of God then you cannot be a sinner. In the latter case, animals, children and non-Christians cannot be called sinners. Venial sins are relatively minor sins which can be 'bought back' with good works or penances but the Seven Deadly Sins (or the Seven Mortal or Capital Sins) are punishable by death (unless they are absolved). These are Pride, Avarice (Greed, Covetousness), Lust, Anger (Wrath), Gluttony, Envy and Sloth. By comparison, the Seven Virtues are Faith, Hope, Charity (these three are the Christian Virtues), Justice, Fortitude, Prudence and Temperance (these are the Cardinal Virtues first put forward, in pre-Christian times, by the Greek Philosopher Plato).

Patron Saints. Some saints have been identified with particular countries, often because they have performed holy deeds or miracles in those places. St David, for example, though little is known of his life, was a priest in Wales who was responsible for moving the seat of ecclesiastical authority in that country from Caerleon-on-Usk to what is now St David's, Powys, and was canonized by Pope Calixtus II in c.1120. His feast day is 1 March.

St Andrew (brother of St Peter) became the patron saint of Scotland because a ship bearing two relics of him was supposed to have been wrecked in St Andrew's Bay, Fife. Some of the mariners managed to reach the shore and introduced Christianity into the then heathen land. His feast day is 30 November.

Ireland's patron saint, St Patrick, originally came from Wales and was the son of a Roman official. He was captured

'He's the Patron Saint of drunks.'

43

by the Picts as a boy and sold into slavery in Ireland but escaped to Gaul. He was later ordained deacon and, landing in Wicklow, set out to convert Ulster and other parts of Ireland to Christianity. He is also reputed to have cleared the country of snakes and chose the shamrock to illustrate to the Irish the doctrine of the Trinity. He died in AD 461 and his feast day is 17 March.

St George is the patron saint of England but there is no clear explanation why this should be so as he was an early Christian martyr in the east, possibly at Lydda in Palestine. Legends about the warrior saint abounded in the 6th century and the story of him rescuing a maiden from a dragon seems to have first appeared in the 12th century, with St George depicted as a youth wearing knights' armour marked with a scarlet cross. The most probable cause for his adoption in England is that he was reputedly seen in a vision helping the Crusaders at the siege of Antioch in 1098. His feast day is 23 April. Other national patron saints include St Denis (France), St Olaf (Norway) and St Joseph (Belgium). Because of their association with various holy deeds there are also patron saints of professions and trades, for example St Christopher (travellers – legend has it he carried Christ across a river), St Luke (artists – he reputedly painted a picture of the Virgin Mary), St Jerome (librarians – he compiled the Vulgate version of the Bible) and so forth.

'She's washing her hair tonight.'

The Apostles. The Greek word *apostolos* means 'a messenger' ('missionary' comes from the equivalent Latin root) but only a few of Jesus's many disciples were called apostles, including the 12 particularly close followers who were selected to go out and spread the word of Christianity throughout the world, preaching repentance and healing the sick. Of these 12, all except Judas Iscariot (who was from Judaea) came from Jesus's own province of Galilee and some (like Peter) were married. The first two he chose as apostles were the former disciples of John the Baptist – the fishermen Andrew and his brother Simon. The latter – who also wrote two of the books in the New Testament – was the most eminent of Jesus's disciples (along with Paul) and he renamed him Cephas (Hebrew for 'a rock') or Petros (Peter) – the Greek equivalent – as he was to be the rock on which the new church would be built. The next two apostles were also fishermen, James and his brother John (author of the fourth Gospel, three epistles and the Book of Revelation), then came Philip and his friend Bartholomew (also called Nathanael). After him was Matthew (a tax-gatherer for the Roman government) who wrote one of the four synoptic Gospels. Next was Thomas, best known as 'doubting Thomas' for his scepticism about Jesus's resurrection (he was convinced when he touched his wounds), then Jesus's 'cousin' James the Less, the son of Alphaeus (Alphaeus's wife may have been the Virgin Mary's sister) and author of the Epistle of James. The last three were Simon the Zealot (a fanatical Jewish sect), Judas (also known as Thaddaeus) – the brother of James the Less (and hence another cousin of Jesus) and the writer of the epistle of Jude – and finally Judas Iscariot, who was the group's treasurer and who betrayed Jesus for 'thirty pieces of silver'. Most of the apostles died unnatural deaths: Andrew (crucified on an X-shaped cross in Greece), Peter (crucified by Nero, allegedly

'Listen, I saw him in the Gospel according to St Matthew.
He was BRILLIANT in that one!'

head-downwards at his own request in Rome c.AD 66), James (killed by sword c.AD 44 in Palestine, the first apostle to be martyred), Thomas (pierced by a lance in India), Matthew (killed with a halberd at Nabadar), Jude (killed with a club), James the Less (hit on the head by a pole), Matthias (stoned then beheaded with a battleaxe), Philip (hanged by the neck from a pillar), Simon (sawn to death), Bartholomew (flayed with a knife) and Judas Iscariot (suicide by hanging in Jerusalem). Paul, who hadn't personally known Jesus when alive but who was, with Peter, the most important of all the apostles, was called the Apostle to the Gentiles or Goyim (non-Jews) as the others only preached to Jews. He was martyred in Rome (beheaded with a sword). (See also SPREADING THE WORD.)

Some Notable Martyrs. *Martyr* is the Greek word for a witness or one who bears testimony, and thus is also used for those who die for their faith. In his *The Book of Martyrs* (1559) John Foxe traced the history of martyrdom from earliest times but made especial reference to the Protestants killed during the reign of the Catholic Mary I of England ('Bloody Mary'). The first ever Christian martyr was St Stephen, one of the most important early Christians before Paul's conversion, who was accused of blasphemy and was stoned to death by a mob. And the first Christian martyr in Britain was St Alban, a Roman soldier who was beheaded *c*.AD 305 on a hill overlooking the Roman town of Verulamium (now St Albans, Hertfordshire) for harbouring a Christian priest during their persecution in the reign of Emperor Diocletian. Another who died during this empire-wide purge was St Sebastian. He was reputedly a Roman army captain who converted many soldiers to Christianity and was condemned to be tied to a tree and shot to death by archers in Rome in AD 288. St Catherine was a very learned young girl of the nobility in Alexandria, Egypt, in the 4th century, and a virgin. She protested against the persecutions of the Christians under the Emperor Maxentius, defeated secular philosophers at a public debate, and was tied to a wheel in punishment. When, miraculously, the fetters broke, she was beheaded.

'We decided to let him off with a warning this time!'

Heretics and The Inquisition. A heretic is someone who holds theological views that are not the orthodox ones and thus in the eyes of those in the mainstream of Christianity. He is often seen as a sinner and is excommunicated or executed as such. The original formulation of Christian orthodoxy, reputedly based on the doctrine taught by the Apostles themselves, was the 2nd-century Apostles' Creed (*credo* is Latin for 'I believe'). This was refined in the Nicene Creed issued in 325 at the Council of Nicaea, Bithynia (now part of Turkey). The earliest heretics were the Ebionites (from *ebion*, Hebrew for 'poor') who were, like the Apostles (who only preached to Jews), Jewish Christians and kept the Sabbath as well as the Lord's Day (Sunday). They were classed as heretical in the 2nd century when it was agreed that the Christian movement should be universal. Next came the Gnostics (Greek *gnosis* means 'knowledge'), who believed that they had personal mystic knowledge of salvation, and later came the Manichaeans (who, for nine years,

included in their number St Augustine) – followers of Mani who held that darkness is co-existent with light and God. The Arians, who believed amongst other things that Jesus was distinct from God, followed Arius of Alexandria. In the Middle Ages various other sects arose such as the Waldensians (followers of Peter Waldo of Lyons) who rejected the papacy and returned to the teaching of the Gospels, and the Albigensians (from the city of Albi in Languedoc) in the 12th and 13th centuries. It was the growth of the latter which led to the establishment of an ecclestiastical court known as The Inquisition in 1231 run by Dominican and Franciscan monks, its procedure being known as *auto-da-fé* (Portuguese for 'act of faith'). Victims were burnt at the stake because the Inquisitors were forbidden to shed blood (a notable martyr being Joan of Arc). The famous Spanish Inquisition under its first Grand Inquisitor Torquemada was established in 1479 and during his term of office 2000 heretics were burnt. Many Protestant Christians were also

executed as heretics in the 16th century, notably the Huguenots in France (50,000 being slaughtered on St Bartholomew's Day 1572 alone) and under Mary I ('Bloody Mary') in England (including Thomas Cranmer, Archbishop of Canterbury and instigator of the Book of Common Prayer, and William Tyndale, translator of the Bible into English).

*'Tyndale's not on till three –
I'm just the warm-up act.'*

Witchcraft, Black Magic and Dr Faustus.
The practice of sorcery (witchcraft comes from *wiccian*, Old English for 'sorcery', and 'sorcery' itself comes from the Old French word meaning 'a caster of lots') was severely suppressed by the Inquisition following an edict of 1484 by Pope Innocent VIII. It was made a felony in England in 1542, and causing death by witchcraft was decreed a capital offence in 1563. Many old women died as a result of these purges. Dr Johann Faust, who came from Württemberg in Germany and died c.1538, acquired a reputation for evil and reputedly had supernatural powers. Based on *The History of Dr Faustus, the Notorious Magician and Master of the Black Art*, published in Frankfurt in 1587, the legend grew. Both Marlowe and Goethe wrote famous books on the character in which he is seen as making a pact with the Devil, selling his soul to him in exchange for 24 years of life during which he is able to experience all pleasure and all knowledge. At the end of the 24 years, however, the Devil claims his reward . . .

RULES AND RITES

Christian Law and Traditions

The original rules and regulations of the Christian Church were based on the Law of Moses outlined in the Old Testament books of Exodus, Leviticus and Deuteronomy. Many of the detailed regulations about sacrifices, unclean meats, circumcision, etc., though still relevant to Judaism, were waived when Christianity was introduced to the Gentiles (non-Jews) but the moral code as exemplified in the 10 Commandments is still a central tenet of the faith. However, exactly when other laws should be followed and the precise manner in which they are carried out and by whom has led to considerable controversy over the centuries and produced a number of divisions in the Church. Nowadays, the main rulings centre on baptism, confirmation, marriage and death, confession and absolution, Holy Communion, fasting and food regulations, birth and contraception, and the use of prayer and song.

The 10 Commandments

The 10 Commandments or Decalogue were originally very short (decalogue means literally '10 words' in Greek) and were the sort of rules common in most communities in the ancient world at that time. As detailed in Exodus Chapter XX they read as follows (the wording is slightly different when they are repeated in Deuteronomy Chapter V): i) 'Thou shalt have no other gods before me'; ii) 'Thou shalt not make unto thee any graven image, or any likeness of any thing that is in heaven above or that is in the earth beneath or that is in the water under the earth. Thou shalt not bow down thyself to them [i.e. the images] nor serve them...'; iii) 'Thou shalt not take the name of the Lord thy God in vain...'; iv) 'Remember the Sabbath Day, to keep it Holy...'; v) 'Honour thy father and thy mother...'; vi) 'Thou shalt not kill'; vii) 'Thou shalt not commit adultery'; viii) 'Thou shalt not steal'; ix) 'Thou shalt not bear false witness against thy neighbour'; and x) 'Thou shalt not covet thy neighbour's house... wife... manservant... maidservant, nor his ox, nor his ass, nor anything that is thy neighbour's.'

The Stone Tablets. After leading the Israelites across the Red Sea en route for the Promised Land of Canaan (Palestine), Moses paused at the foot of Mt Sinai on the eastern perimeter of Egypt where he and the Chosen People heard the voice of God and the terms of his covenant with them. Covenants were familar from earlier times and effectively laid down the obligations that a vassal ruler of a smaller state had to his sovereign king, binding the two together. The contract was then witnessed and deposited in a safe place. Once God had pronouced the terms of his covenant to Moses, witnessed by the people, Moses went up into the mountain and returned with the essential items written 'by the finger of the Lord' on both sides of two stone tablets. These were later placed in the chest known as the Ark of the Covenant and carried around with the Israelites until finding their resting pace in the Temple in Jerusalem.

Baptism. Most religions in history have included a purification ceremony involving the ritual washing of adults or infants. However, the Christian act of baptism or christening ('making Christian') derives specifically from the practices of Jesus's contemporary John the Baptist who immersed penitents in the River Jordan to cleanse them of their sins and who even baptized Jesus himself when a young man. Later, though, when Jesus instructed his Apostles regarding the practice of baptism (he never performed the ritual himself), it was not only to wash away evil but also to confer the gift of the Holy Spirit for without this entry to Heaven was impossible – 'Until one is born of water and the Spirit, he cannot enter the kingdom of heaven.' Their

'Blimey, you're early'

subjects, however, were originally mostly adults, who were first instructed in the faith and then would prepare for the rite by prayer, confession and swearing to abjure the Devil before being immersed in water – either in a spring, a river, or (later) a large tank – three times. Later 'infusion' (pouring water on the head) and 'aspersion' (sprinkling) became popular in the West and by the 2nd century the baptism of infants was common. To house the tank in early churches a separate baptistery was built but later a smaller receptacle known as a font (Latin for 'spring') replaced the tank and baptistries themselves disappeared, the font merely being situated inside the church near the door to symbolize the entry into Christian life.

Confirmation. When the baptism of children became more widespread, the new ritual of confirmation was introduced. In Anglican practice, a baptised person who has reached the age of reason (usually from the age of 11 upwards) is instructed in the basic principles of Christianity and then presented to a bishop who anoints the candidate on the forehead with the sign of the cross in a formal ceremony. In many churches confirmation is a prerequisite for receiving Holy Communion.

Holy Communion. Paul gave the name 'the Lord's Supper' to the custom Jesus instituted on the evening before his execution. In the original version it was a variant of the standard Jewish Passover meal (celebrating the Israelites' deliverance from the Plague which killed the first-born of the Egyptians) which Jesus and the Apostles were observing in the normal manner. However, when it came to the eating of the stipulated unleavened bread and the drinking of the watered-down wine (the sacrificial male lamb or kid having already been consumed) Jesus suddenly declared that these two items were henceforth to represent his body and his blood respectively, and asked his disciples to repeat this new ordinance in his memory once he had died. The ceremony (minus the other Jewish Passover elements such as the lamb and the daubing of blood on doorposts, etc.) has since been regularly carried out every Sunday by Christians worldwide and is also known as the Eucharist (from the Greek word meaning 'grateful' or 'a thanksgiving').

Marriage and Weddings. The word 'marry' comes from the Latin *maritus* ('a husband') and 'wedding' is Old English for 'a covenant'. The first biblical husband and wife were Adam and Eve in the Garden of Eden. Apart from exceptions such as Abraham, Jacob, David and Solomon, the Bible largely promotes monogamy and this is the current Christian ruling. The modern Church ceremony in which the partners 'plight their troth' (or pledge their word of truth) has taken many forms, but the act of the man placing a ring on the fourth finger of his betrothed's hand has been constant. The ring symbolizes the man's pledge but in Britain has only been put on the woman's left hand since the 16th century (hitherto the right had been used). The fourth finger is significant apparently because it was believed that a nerve or

Wedding Cakes and Confetti
The multi-tiered traditional wedding cake (iced in white) originated with a confectioner who lived near St Bride's Church in London's Fleet Street and who copied the design of the church's three-tiered tower. Corn used to be thrown over the newly married couple on the church steps, symbolizing fertility, but nowadays it is mostly rice (from a similar Hindu practice) or confetti, from the Italian word for 'comfits' or 'sweets', which used to be thrown at Carnival time. Nowadays, the confetti usually consists of paper charms such as horseshoes, hearts, etc.

vein known as the *vena amoris* flowed from that finger directly to the heart. White clothes are worn by the bride to symbolize purity and virginity.

'You DO!!'

Prayer and Confession. In prayer, the petitioner humbly addresses God in praise, thanksgiving, confession of sins or else in entreaty to grant requests. Prayer can be silent and individual, or spoken or sung out loud by a group or congregation conducted by a priest. All religions from ancient times to the present day have used prayer and many also have formulae which are believed to be effective if repeated often enough. Tibetan Buddhists make use of prayer-wheels to assist their devotions and others use lighted candles or tapers etc. A Roman Catholic aid is the rosary – a string of 55 or 165 beads used to help count 5 or 15 decades of Aves (short for 'Ave Maria' or 'Hail Mary') – the small beads – each beginning with a Paternoster (the Lord's Prayer in Latin) – a large bead – and ending with a Gloria (*Gloria in Excelsis Deo*, 'Glory be to God in the Highest') – a large bead. Reciting various numbers of these prayers (the amount fixed by a priest according to the gravity of one's sin) by 'telling' beads on the rosary is also one of the penances which follow the absolution of sins. These penances are given out by a priest after hearing a penitent's sins spoken anonymously through a grille dividing two compartments in one of the specially designed curtained booths known as 'confessional boxes' which are placed for this purpose in Catholic churches.

'Nothing I can do, I'm afraid – it's an occupational hazard...'

Prayer. These two books comprise the main two reference works of modern Church of England Christianity. The latter contains the approved liturgy for use in Anglican worship and was a direct product of the Reformation, being introduced and largely written by Henry's VIII's first

Archbishop of Canterbury, Thomas Cranmer in 1549. The Bible itself, though literally 'the Book', is in fact a collection of books grouped in two sections as the Old Testament (which is also one of the main texts of Judaism) and the New Testament, outlining the life and works of Jesus and the acts of the Apostles etc. The Old Testament is traditionally divided into three parts: the Pentateuch

Deuteronomy allegedly written by Moses and also known as the Torah or 'Law' in Judaism); the Prophets (21 books); and the Hagiographa (general sacred works such as Proverbs, Psalms etc.). A collection of disputed works (usually published as a separate volume) is the Apocrypha. The New Testament is divided into the four Gospels, Acts of the Apostles, the Epistles and Revelation. These texts were originally written as continuous scrolls in three languages – Hebrew (most of the Old Testament), Greek and Aramaic – and weren't separated into verses until the 9th century and into chapters until the 13th century (the first complete version of the modern layout being the Geneva Bible of 1560). The first translation of the Bible (in fact the first translation of any book to be written down) was the Greek version of the Old Testament known as the Septuagint – so-called because legend has it that it was compiled by 70 scholars in the 2nd and 3rd centuries BC. The first complete translation of the whole Bible (into Latin) – and the first book of any kind ever printed – was the Vulgate compiled by St Jerome in AD 404 and still in use to this day. Then came English versions by William Tyndale (translated from the original Greek and Hebrew texts) and the familiar Authorized or King James Version of 1611. Since the 19th-century new versions have multiplied prolifically.

Exorcism. The ceremony of exorcism is essentially that of casting out demons from people who have become 'possessed' and was practised by Jesus himself. In the 3rd century a special branch of the clergy was formed to carry out this function. Ordinary priests may still carry out exorcism – most commonly in the case of haunted houses nowadays – but only with special authorization from a bishop.

Funerals. In the early centuries of Christianity, funerals were happy occasions and people dressed in white in joy that the deceased was going to meet Jesus in Heaven. But by the 8th century it had become a ritual of mourning and the wearing of black became widespread. In the Roman Catholic Church, at the approach of death a priest visits the dying person to hear confession, absolve sins and administer both Holy Communion and Extreme Unction (anointing with olive oil which has been blessed by a bishop). The priest then prays and after death a requiem mass may be held. Deceased Catholics are usually buried but others are frequently cremated nowadays. In interment the body is laid flat in a coffin and buried with the feet facing east, ready to rise and meet Jesus when he appears again on the Mount of Olives in Jerusalem. A cross or inscribed headstone is erected at the head of the body. If a person dies aboard ship the body is usually cast into the sea.

FESTIVALS AND HOLY DAYS

The Church Year

The traditional Church year is divided up into a number of festivals and holy days (from which we get the word 'holiday') to do with the life of Jesus and the saints. Many of these are officially sanctioned by governments as days when people are not required to work (bank holidays, when even the banks close). However, very few of these special days existed much before the 3rd or 4th centuries and a number were deliberately merged with earlier pagan or Jewish festivals to gain popular appeal when they were first introduced. In addition, different branches of Christianity – Eastern Orthodox, Catholic, Anglican, Lutheran etc. – give different emphasis to certain festivals and holy days and in some cases even celebrate them on different days. The main Christian festivals are Christmas, Epiphany, Good Friday, Easter, Ascension and Pentecost/Whitsunday. The last four of these are movable feasts and depend on when the first full moon occurs after the spring equinox.

Christmas Customs and Santa Claus

Customs such as the giving of wrapped-up gifts, feasting, wassailing, burning of logs, the erection of indoor fir-trees with fairy lights etc., all derive from earlier pagan celebrations such as the Roman Saturnalia (17–24 December) and the North European Yuletide festivals. Father Christmas himself, called Santa Claus in the USA by a corruption of the name St Nicholas (Sinterklaas in Dutch), only became associated with the Nativity festival in comparatively recent times, as the martyred bishop's saints' day is actually 6 December. However, as it was traditional to give presents in honour of the legend that St Nicholas secretly gave dowry donations to three daughters of a poor citizen to save them from destitution (the three bags of gold allegedly inspiring the three gold balls of the pawnbroker's symbol), this too has been mixed in and the customs merged into one big jolly beano (indeed, Christmas now even seems to be threatening to join up with the New Year celebrations with many offices closing for the entire festive season). Santa Claus's appearance as a fat, jovial, bearded old man dressed in a red habit and hood trimmed in white was entirely the creation of the 19th-century American cartoonist Thomas Nast (in Europe, St Nicholas is traditionally dressed completely differently and carries birch twigs to beat naughty children as well as presents for the good ones).

Christmas and Epiphany. Christmas and Epiphany are the two fixed dates in the Christian Year, 25 December and 6 January respectively. Neither have any historical accuracy with regard to Jesus's life and indeed both were timed to coincide with popular pagan celebrations of the winter solstice. Christmas (the mass for Christ) is a feast supposedly celebrating the nativity of Jesus but was not actually established as such until at least the 4th century, and then only in Rome. At that time it was merged with another festival, that of the birthday of the unconquered Sun (from the winter solstice the sun's light gets progressively stronger). However, Christmas wasn't celebrated on 25 December in Jerusalem (or many other places) until the 6th century, Jesus's birth until then having been commemorated as part of the much earlier Christian festival of Epiphany (from the Greek word for 'manifestation' – i.e. the manifestation of God as Jesus both to the Magi and in Christ's baptism in the River Jordan). Exactly when the historical Jesus was born is still unclear. It is now commonly held that it was most likely to have been some six to eight years earlier than the traditional date and probably in the autumn, not winter.

GOODBYE – SEE YOU AT EASTER!"

'I don't know why we even bother trying to go away at Easter.'

Eastertide, Lent and Whitsun. Apart from observance of the Lord's Day on Sundays, Easter is the oldest of the Christian festivals and is the most important, celebrating as it does the death and resurrection of Jesus. Easter Sunday (the day of the Resurrection) originally fell on the second day of the Jewish festival of Passover and as the Jewish calendar was based on lunar months this meant that some years it would fall on a weekday. As a result – and after years of disagreement (running well into the 7th century) by various factions in the world's Christian community who used different calendar systems – it now falls on the first Sunday following the first full moon after the spring equinox (21 March). The run-up to Easter begins with Lent – formerly the name for the season of spring itself (Lent derives from the word for 'long') – a once strict 40-day period of fasting symbolizing Jesus's 40 days in the wilderness and beginning with Ash Wednesday (so-called because penitents used to heap ash on their heads). This is traditionally preceded by Shrove Tuesday (when Christians would go to confession and thereby be shriven of their sins) on which scraps of food would be finished up (hence pancakes) prior to the fast. Nowadays many find it sufficient just to give up some item of food or some favoured activity. The fourth Sunday in Lent is known as Mothering Sunday (Mother's Day in the USA, founded in 1907, is celebrated in May) when children traditionally visit and give presents to their mothers, though this has no biblical connotation. Whitsun (White Sunday) is when the Holy Spirit descended on the Apostles and gave them the 'gift of tongues', allowing them to talk the language of foreign nations and thus promote the Christian message abroad. This latter day is also called Pentecost, meaning the 50th day, as it was a Jewish feast marking the 50th day after Passover (also the 50th day after Jesus's resurrection). The name 'Easter' derives from Eostre, the pagan goddess of the dawn (which also gives us the name of the compass-point 'east'). Easter eggs and Easter bunnies are both reminders of earlier fertility festivals and have nothing to do with Christianity.

'It's easy, Father ... just like ... er ... well I was going to say ... tying a tie.'

Harvest Festival. The harvest festival is a tradition that has been held in most countries and celebrated in all religions from time immemorial. The Christianized version of the Jewish festival has the church decorated with fruit, grain, vegetables, loaves of bread etc. while a service of thanksgiving is held. The exact date in the autumn is movable and depends on when the harvest has actually been gathered in. In bygone times a 'harvest-home' supper would also be held and a goose would be served.

'By the way, George – if you're thinking of making the same Harvest Festival offering as last year, could you leave it OUTSIDE the church?'

Hallowe'en, All Saints' Day and All Souls' Day. Hallowe'en – strictly All Hallows' Even – on 31 October takes its name from the following day, All Saints' Day (1 November) in that to hallow means to venerate someone as holy and in fact derives from the word 'holy' itself. It is thus literally the evening before All Saints' Day. Instituted by Pope Gregory III when he created a chapel to all the saints in St Peter's, Rome, it was made into a general church festival by Gregory IV in 834. However, there are close links with the earlier Roman harvest festival of Pomona and with Druidism. This latter connection is very strong as the Celtic year ended on 31 October and was celebrated by the feast of Samhain in which the spirits of the dead would visit their families in search of warmth as winter approached. The building of bonfires to guide them and at the same time to ward off evil spirits has largely been absorbed into the activities of Guy Fawkes Night (5 November) in Britain. However, the pagan night of the dead with its witches, black cats, skeletons and bonfires was taken to America with the Founding Fathers and thus (not having an interest in Guy Fawkes) Hallowe'en is a much more important festival there. In the Roman Catholic Church the day after All Saints' Day – during which the blessed dead in Heaven are praised – is All Souls' Day when prayers are given up to and requiem masses are held for those unfortunates who have died and are still trapped in Purgatory.

'What do you mean, I can remove my mask now? – What mask?'

MONKS AND NUNS

Monasticism

The austere and devout lifestyle of the ascetic and mystic was originally developed centuries before the birth of Jesus in ancient India and Asia and was also practised in different ways by various schools of Greek Philosophy such as the Orphics, Cynics and Stoics. Indeed, the word 'monk' itself comes from the Greek *monachos* meaning 'solitary', and is derived from *monos* meaning 'alone' or 'single'. The original Christian monk – in fact a hermit – was St Anthony, but the first true Christian monastery or cenobium (meaning 'common life') was that established at Tabennisi near Dendera, Egypt, by St Pachomius in AD 323. By the time of his death he had set up 10 monasteries (one of them for women) and by AD 410 this, the first ever religious 'order', numbered some 7000 monks and nuns in southern Egypt and northern Ethiopia. The monastic movement then spread quickly abroad with the work of St Basil, St Benedict, St Jerome and others. By the time of the Reformation in the 16th century, the monasteries in England had become very wealthy and held a strong allegiance to the Pope. As a result, when Henry VIII broke away from Rome after the Pope had refused to sanction his divorce from Katherine of Aragon in order to marry Anne Boleyn – and set up the Church of England with himself as its head – he forcibly closed down or destroyed most of the cenobia in a move that has become known as the Dissolution of the Monasteries.

'This is Roger, our deep, fat friar!'

St Anthony and the Hermit Tradition.

A hermit (usually male) is one who isolates himself from the rest of the world in order to have closer communion with God. The word itself comes from the Greek for desert and the home of a hermit is known as a hermitage. The first Christian hermit was also the first ever Christian monk. His name was St Anthony and he was born in Egypt c.AD 250. He began to practise the ascetic life at the age of 20 and 15 years later became a hermit on a mountain near the River Nile and eventually withdrew to another peak near the Red Sea where now stands a monastery in his name. He is best known for his frequent encounters with the forces of evil in the forms of women, wild beasts and soldiers who constantly tempted him to leave his difficult way of life. St Anthony died in AD 355 and his feast day is 17 January. Another class of hermits were the Stylites who took their name from St Simeon Stylites of Syria (390–459) who spent 30 years seated on a pillar (Greek *stulos*) 60 feet high without descending. These pillar-saints were found mostly in Syria, Mesopotamia, Egypt and Greece between the 5th and 10th centuries.

'Your tea's ready.'

Mendicant Friars. Though like monks in general, mendicant (or begging) holy men had existed in ancient times, the first Christian orders living entirely on public alms were founded in Western Europe by the Spaniard St Dominic and the Italian St Francis of Assisi, who both died in the first half of the 13th century. They were called 'friars' after the French word *frère* meaning a brother. The four main orders were distinguished by the colour of their dress, which consisted of a simple garment known as a 'habit'. These were the Black Friars (Dominican, who also wore a rosary – which they popularized – on their girdles), White Friars (Carmelite), Grey Friars (Franciscan, who also wore brown – of which a sub-order were the Capuchins who wore a *cappuccio* or pointed cowl) and the Austin Friars (Augustinian, who also dressed in black, and were named after St Augustine who brought Christianity to Britain). The Carmelites took their name from Mt Carmel in Israel,

'They'll always change it for you if it fits.'

famed for its association with the prophet Elijah, and a sub-group founded by St Teresa in the 16th century didn't wear shoes. Several other orders flourished for a while but all except these four were suppressed by the Council of Lyons in 1274. The friars, who catered to the needs of the poor and themselves lived a life of austerity with little personal property, became popular at a time when the public were becoming unhappy at the increasing wealth of the monasteries and Cathedrals.

'Lights out, Brother Dominic.'

St Francis. St Francis of Assisi was the founder of the Franciscan order of mendicant monks and is the patron saint of Italy. He was born in Assisi, Umbria, *c*.1181 and had a vision at Spoleto while serving in the army. He renounced material goods and his family and, wearing only a hair shirt, lived in the woods of Mt Subasio before becoming an itinerant preacher. He saw all nature as a mirror of God and was a great lover of nature, especially birds. He was also the first and most celebrated person to have received the holy stigmata (marks made by a pointed instrument) – his hands, feet and left side having, while

'Brother Francis from Assisi, I presume.'

praying one day, received the same wounds as Jesus on the Cross.

Tonsures. The practice of shaving a part of the head became customary amongst monks in the 6th and 7th centuries. The usual form involved shaving the crown and leaving a circlet of hair to symbolize Jesus's 'crown of thorns'. However, there was also a Celtic version where hair was shaved from the front of the head back to a line over the skull extending from ear to ear. And in the Greek Orthodox Church the head was shaved completely bald.

Nuns. The word 'nun' comes from the Latin *nonnus* for a monk (*nonna* being the female variant). Virgins have always played a part in religious communities, from sacrifices to temple guardians (as in the Roman Vestal Virgins). One of the earliest Christian nuns was the sister of St Anthony himself, and each of the sisters of the founders of the great monastic orders – St Pachomius, St Basil and St Benedict – also founded female lines of those orders and set up nunneries. Seen as 'Brides of Christ', they were vowed to chastity and poverty. There were also female hermits and friars, known as 'Poor Clares'. These latter were named after their founder, St Clare, who was a follower of St Francis of Assisi in the 13th century. However, most of the modern nuns follow the Augustinian rule. In 1633 St Vincent de Paul established the Sisters of Charity who were not confined to nunneries but allowed to nurse in hospitals and to help in school education. The dress of nuns tends to reflect that of their male counterparts except that they usually also wear a wimple over their heads.

Silent Orders. One of the most penitential of the monastic orders is that of the Trappists, a Cistercian group based originally at the abbey of La Trappe near Soligny, Normandy. It was ruled by a converted courtier, Armand Jean le Bouthillier de Rancé, from 1664 and he introduced a very rigorous regime that went far beyond the rules of St Benedict and the Cistercians. Despite the harsh regulations, which included penitential exercises, an austere diet – living only on bread, vegetables, fruit and a little cheese and milk – and a vow of absolute silence, the abbey had 300 monks in de Rancé's own time and there are now Trappist monasteries in Europe, America, Asia and the Far East. The Belgian Trappists are also well-known for brewing a particularly strong variety of beer.

'...and this is the ruined Abbot!'

St Benedict, St Bruno and Booze.

St Benedict was born in Nusia, near Spoleto, Italy, *c.*480 and as a young man spent three years as a hermit in a cave opposite Nero's palace at Subiaco (near Rome) before founding his order with 12 monasteries in the area. He then moved to Monte Cassino, midway between Rome and Naples, and founded the famous abbey which was destroyed by the Allies in World War II. The Benedictine rule was far from austere and other groups – such as the Cistercians (named after Cîteaux in Burgundy) – also followed it. The prime monastic order devoted to learning and literature, it is also celebrated for its abbey at Cluny, France (whose church was the largest in Europe prior to the re-building of St Peter's, Rome), and for creating in 1510 the brandy-based herb-and-honey liqueur Bendectine D.O.M. (standing for *Deo Optimo Maximo* – 'To God, most good, most great'). Another powerful liqueur, distilled by the Carthusians, is Chartreuse which is made from 130 different herbs and comes in two varieties, green (55% alcohol) and yellow (43%). The name comes from the Chartreuse valley near Grenoble in France where St Bruno first founded the order in 1084 (the British 'Charterhouse' is an anglicized version of the name).

'First it became unsafe to have cigarettes, then sex, then food, then water – so I thought, what's left?'

Literature and Christianity. Most of early literature from the collapse of the Roman Empire in the 5th century was written by clerics – usually monks – as very few could read or write, let alone in Latin which was the *lingua franca* until the 14th century. (For the connection between clerics and clerks see THE CLERGY.) Books in Ancient Greek and Roman times followed the Egyptian tradition and were written on papyrus scrolls about 9 inches wide and 35 feet long (though some – such as the Dead Sea Scrolls – were made of leather). Later came the codex (from *caudex* meaning 'a tree-trunk or tablet') or modern form of book with folded leaves bound together along one edge – thereby allowing writing on both sides of the leaves and much easier access to the text – and from the 4th century onwards the codex form was dominant. Codices were made at first of the much more durable vellum or parchment (finely shaved animal skins) – though some were also of papyrus – but by the 15th century paper manuscripts were the norm. The scribes in monasteries largely concentrated on copying out the Bible or making commentaries on the Scriptures but a considerable amount of scientific, medical and historical writing was also done. In addition, a tradition of lavish decoration of books known as 'illuminated manuscripts' grew up from about the 6th century and flourished in the Middle Ages until the Renaissance. Noteworthy examples are the Irish *Book of Kells*, the Carolingian *Utrecht Psalter* and the French *Très Riches Heures du Duc de Berry*. The German Gutenberg Bible (1454) – the world's first book printed from movable type – was also highly illuminated to disguise the fact that the text had not been hand-copied.

'Sorry, Guv. Office party.'

THE CLERGY

Clergy and Laity

We get the modern word 'clergy' from the Greek word *kleros* meaning a 'lot' or 'heritage'. In the Bible the Levites (one of the orders of Jewish priesthood) were called 'God's heritage' and hence Christian ministers also became known as clerks or clerics. And, as all business involving writing was originally done by monks and other scholars in holy orders, a clerk later came to be seen as anyone who was in charge of records and writing in business, court etc. The religious officers subsequently became better known as 'clergymen' or 'the clergy' and generally it applies to all from the highest to the lowest. The clergy, then, are distinguished from the laity (Greek *laos*, the people) and, being rulers over our souls as opposed to our bodies, have over the centuries been allowed certain exemptions in criminal law. Indeed, 'benefit of clergy', introduced in the 12th century, stated that clergymen were immune to prosecution and punishment in lay courts and could only be tried by ecclesiastical courts (which never inflicted the death penalty). By the 14th century, even laymen convicted of capital offences could escape death this way if they passed a test (usually reciting the first verse of Psalm 51) and could thereby claim clerical immunity. (The playwright Ben Jonson was branded on the thumb as proof of his release in this manner.) Benefit of clergy was later also extended to women and illiterates, but with the practice of transporting overseas those guilty of capital offences it fell into decline and was eventually abolished in 1827. Other special dispensations for clergy include exemption from jury service and from candidature for election to the House of Commons (though bishops – 'Lords Spiritual' – sit in the House of Lords).

*'It's a holy-water cannon...
just in case the theology students
get restive...'*

The Pope. The name for the leader of the Roman Catholic Church comes from the Greek *pappas* meaning 'father' but was not used officially until the 5th century (by Pope Leo the Great) and even then was not exclusively reserved for the bishop of Rome until the 11th century. Hitherto, spiritual leaders in the Christian Church had been known only as bishops (from the Greek *episkopos* meaning, literally, 'an overseer'). The primacy of Rome as the centre of the Church was also not immediate. After the persecutions of Christians in Jerusalem following the martyrdom of St Stephen, many fled to the largely non-Jewish city of Antioch in Syria (the third largest city in the Roman Empire after Rome and Alexandria). It was here that the disciples were first called 'Christians' and it was from here that Paul and others set out on their missionary journeys. However, it would be at Rome that St Peter met his death (as did Paul) and it was Peter (formerly named Simon) upon whom Jesus had conferred the name 'the Rock' (Greek *petros*) as it would be on him that the Church would be founded. Peter was to be the vicar ('substitute') of God on earth after Jesus's death. The Pope's title 'pontiff' comes from the Latin *pontifex* (bridge-maker) – a member of the main college of priests in Ancient Rome. Popes have come from many countries (including one from England, Nicholas Breakspear [Adrian IV]) but the majority have been Italian. The tradition of changing the Pope's Christian name first arose with Sergius II in the 9th century as his name was Peter and out of respect for the Apostle there has never been a Peter II.

Cardinals and the Curia. The ecclesiastical organization of which the Pope is the head is known as the Curia (the name formerly given to Ancient Roman senates and courthouses). This itself is governed by the College of Cardinals. Originally exclusively drawn from members of the clergy of Rome it now comprises 136 cardinals (all of whom are consecrated bishops) from all over the world. Any new Pope is elected by the College of Cardinals and must already be one of their number.

The word 'cardinal' itself comes from the word for 'a hinge' and thus 'that upon which things depend'. It originally described the parish church itself but by degrees has come to mean the Pope's personal council (since the 16th century), many of whose members have exerted great power in their own countries (e.g. France's Cardinal Richelieu). The distinctive red hat of the cardinal was first introduced in 1245.

Addendum: '. . . and on the eighth day, he made bishops and cardinals after their kind.'

'I've always had my doubts about Jackson.'

Holy Orders. The lowest grade of clergy is the curate (a curer of souls), who helps the fully ordained priest in his work. Above the curate come the deacon and subdeacon, who normally help the priest in church services, and the priest himself, who is granted the power to perform most of the rituals of the Christian church except those of confirmation, consecration and the ordination of priests. He is also known as a pastor (Latin for 'shepherd'), parson (a corruption of 'person') or vicar (one who deputizes). A vicar is seen as not only representing or deputizing for God but also as doing so for the local rector (Latin for 'a ruler') who used to collect compulsory Church taxes ('tithes') from the farmers which amounted to ⅟₁₀ of the

area's produce. Above the priest is the bishop (or prelate) who is the overseer of a diocese. His own administrative centre is a large city church known as a cathedral (from the Latin for 'a seat') – indeed a town becomes a city if it has a cathedral in it. The ecclesiastical staff of a cathedral are the dean (from Latin *decanus* 'one set over 10') and his 'chapter' of 10 canons – so-called because they would read a chapter from Scripture at their meetings. A dean is also a clergyman who supervises rural priests and reports to an archdeacon, an office immediately below that of bishop. The bishop himself reports to an archbishop (or primate), of which there are two Church of England posts in Britain –

Canterbury (chosen by St Augustine because Kent was the most powerful and civilized Anglo-Saxon kingdom of the time) and York (military capital of the Romans in Britain, from where Constantine was first proclaimed Emperor). In the Orthodox Eastern Church an archbishop is known as a metropolitan and the head of the church is called a patriarch (the name originally given to the five most important bishops in Christendom – at Rome, Jerusalem, Antioch, Alexandria and Constantinople). Relatively recent Orthodox patriarchates include Russia, Romania, Bulgaria, Cyprus, Greece and Poland.

'Sometimes I wish he'd dress up as a cowboy.'

Vestments and Clerical Clothing.
Vestments differ from clerical clothing as a whole in that they are only for ceremonial use. The four main garments all derive not from Judaic temple clothing but from Greek and Roman dress. They are the alb (a large white-linen tunic), the dalmatic (worn by deacons), the cope and the chasuble (a rectangular sleeveless garment with a hole in the middle worn to represent the seamless coat of Jesus). Catholic archbishops also wear a pallium, a sort of narrow white scarf with crosses made from lamb's wool blessed in the church of St Agnese, Rome – none may carry out their religious functions until

they have applied for and received the pallium from the Pope himself. Hats include the pileum or skull-cap, originally created to keep a tonsured skull warm, and the square biretta (usually with a pompom in the centre) which developed from it in the 17th century. In addition there is the bishop's mitre with its two pointed arches which are meant to symbolize the cloven firy tongues of the Holy Spirit which descended on the Apostles at Pentecost, giving them the power to speak in all languages. Bishops (and abbots) also wear rings and carry crosiers – an ornamental shepherds' crook representing his relation to his human flock – and an archbishop carries a similar staff which has

a cross instead of a crook at the end. Priests also wear distinctive back-to-front white clerical collars ('dog-collars') with their daily non-ceremonial clerical dress which usually consists of a long tunic known as a cassock. The colour of this garment – which also used to be common amongst soldiers and horsemen but now only survives in clerical dress – varies according to the rank of the wearer: white for the Pope, red for cardinals, purple for bishops and black for lower ranks. Vestments are usually worn over the cassock. Strict Protestant ministers tend either to avoid clerical garb altogether or to adopt academic robes, sometimes with the addition of Geneva bands (two starched white vertical collars). Many 'progressive clergy' wear casual clothes or suits.

de la Nougerède

'He's Russian Orthodox . . .'

Sex and the Priesthood. Many ancient religions had rulings against sex by members of the priesthood, a case in point being the six Vestal Virgins who tended the sacred flame brought by Aeneas from Troy in the Temple of Vesta in the Forum in Rome – if they lost their virginity before their 30 years of office expired they were buried alive. And monastic sects from the earliest times took vows of chastity (complete abstinence from sex) – nuns even being seen as 'brides of Christ'. However, celibacy, in the strict sense of not being married, was not obligatory in the early years of Christianity and has no basis in the Scriptures. None the less, in the late 4th century Pope Siricius changed all this as it was believed that the priest's role as mediator between mankind and God would be affected if he was encumbered with the cares of a wife and family. The Protestant churches, however, reject the idea entirely. Considerable controversy has arisen in recent years over the issue of gay priests, many contending that though a gay relationship is not strictly one of marriage in the conventional sense and thus a gay priest is not breaking vows of celibacy. Formerly the biblical ban on homosexuality made such a thing unthinkable.

Women in Holy Orders. Despite the fact that the Virgin Mary and female saints have always been venerated and that from medieval times women have held responsible positions in the Church, such as that of abbess, there has always been considerable resistance to women priests in Christianity. One of the many arguments against the ordination of women is that all the Apostles were male and it was Peter who was appointed head of the Church by Jesus himself, the implication being that the tradition of the priesthood right from the very beginning was patriarchal and intentionally so. However, in the Anglican and Protestant denominations at least, the tide has recently begun to turn in favour of women clergy.

'Progressive' Clergy. In an attempt to win back a younger generation to Christianity, a number of moves have been made by some clergy to liven up church services. Reflecting on the mass appeal of 'rave' pop concerts some priests have introduced rock music and stage lighting into their churches and dressed more in tune with contemporary fashion. The results in many cases have been dramatic with huge attendance figures but stalwarts of the Church establishment have frowned on their excesses, criticizing them as 'happy clappy' services which substitute spectacle and showmanship for religion.

'It's a lovely church, Vicar. I expect you'll want to change the curtains.'

'You can't be serious!'

'Oh my God! They've sent us a trendy vicar!'

THE HOUSE OF GOD

The Church

The first word used to describe a church was *ecclesia*, the Ancient Greek name for 'a meeting', especially that of the general assembly of Athens. When used later by Christians it referred at first to any particular congregation, but then later to the Christian movement as a whole and the buildings in which they met. At first, of course, because of persecution both by Jews and Romans, meetings of Christians were held in secret, either at houses of wealthy members or in subterranean catacombs (especially those in Rome), but later purpose-built halls emerged in varying styles which eventually gave rise to the cross-shaped churches with their bell-towers, spires, buttresses, stained-glass windows and organ lofts so familiar today. The word 'church' itself derives from the Greek *kuriakon* meaning 'belonging to the Lord'.

Ecclesiastical Architecture. The first churches took the form of the standard Roman basilica (the word is actually Greek for 'a royal palace') which was used as a courthouse and public meeting-room. Basilicas were usually rectangular in plan with a semi-circular extension known

'Look at that! ... they knock down a perfectly good barrow and build one of those modern monstrosities!'

as an apse at one end, an entrance (sometimes with a porch) at the other and a simple wooden roof. The hall inside comprised a central nave (from the word for 'a ship'), to the left and right of which were aisles separated off by lines of columns. The altar was placed in the centre of the apse where it adjoined the nave and the clergy stood or sat behind this with the public in the nave in front (this was the same sort of arrangement as in the standard Roman courthouse). Later features included the introduction of a screen dividing off the entire sanctuary area from the public – this developed into the chancel (*cancelli* is Latin for 'a screen or grating'), the addition of transepts to give a cruciform appearance and the erection of a campanile or bell-tower.

The Byzantine churches, however, based on earlier temple and tomb designs, had a different shape and a domed roof (a famous example being the 6th-century St Sophia in Istanbul). Western cruciform styles have included the Romanesque (i.e. Roman-like style) with thick walls, little buttressing and rounded arches – Saxon and Norman being the dominant variants in Britain – which lasted until the emergence of Gothic architecture with its pointed arches, flying buttresses and ribbed vaulting producing very high interiors and allowing for large windows as the weight of the roof was not directly supported by the walls. Later styles included the Renaissance, which returned to Roman ideas, the florid Baroque and Rococo, and the revivalist Neo-Classical. In the 20th century, with the introduction of reinforced concrete, steel girders etc., the design of churches has become ever more ambitious.

'I'm well aware that cleanliness is next to godliness... I still don't like the idea of the washroom being built alongside the chapel...'

Altars and Communion Tables

Originally an altar (from the word meaning 'on high') was a flat-topped surface, usually made of stone or wood, on which religious sacrifices were made. However, for Christians it has become the rectangular table or box raised on a platform at the east end of a church on which are placed an altar cloth, candles and a crucifix or cross. During the Eucharist the priest places the Holy Sacraments on its surface. Early Christian altars were improvised in the catacombs of Rome upon tombs of the deceased and as a result Roman Catholic churches insist on altars being made of stone and they also frequently contain relics of saints (in other denominations, by contrast, they are often made of wood and never contain relics). Catholic altars can be situated under a baldachin or canopy supported on four pillars. Altarpieces can sometimes be seen on the altars themselves, comprising images in wood or painted on screens – popular designs being of religious scenes depicted on hinged panels in the form of a diptych (two panels) or triptych (three panels). Behind the altar is the reredos, a large wall decoration or stained-glass window. The cross and candles were not placed on altars until the 11th century.

Lecterns and Pulpits. A lectern is (as its name implies) a sort of reading-desk, and first became popular in the 15th century when large bibles and other heavy religious books were introduced. In the Anglican church, lecterns usually take the shape of an eagle with outstretched wings – across which the book is opened – the whole being mounted on a plinth or pillar. Pulpits, by contrast, are of much earlier origin. Deriving from the Latin word for a scaffold, a pulpit is a raised platform with a enclosed front situated on the north side of the sanctuary and from which a priest delivers his sermon or moral lecture. Usually hexagonal or octagonal in shape, they are mostly of wood but some are made of stone and often have a sounding board above them to help project the speaker's voice.

'They said, "You'll never succeed in that parish."
They said, "You'll never make an impression on
that tight-lipped bunch of Puritans." They said,
"You'll never find the key to the wine cupboard."
Well, two out of three ain't bad.'

'. . . and here endeth
the umpteenth
lesson . . .'

Gargoyles. Whilst the interiors of churches are frequently decorated with statuary of saints, paintings and stained-glass windows, the outsides often feature bizarre carvings known as gargoyles. These are basically decorated waterspouts and are attached at the roof-line to conduct rainfall away from the roof and walls. The word comes from the Old French *gargouille* meaning 'a throat' as the water is literally discharged through the throat of the figures. Gargoyles existed in Ancient Rome in the form of lions' heads, but they are now associated largely with the medieval church grotesques featuring fantastical beasts – often birds – and hideous human figure-heads.

Chapels. The word 'chapel' comes from *capella* meaning a small cloak and referred originally to the remaining half of the cloak of St Martin, the famous 4th-century Bishop of Tours and father of French monasticism who, when a soldier, had given the other half to a naked beggar (Martin's subsequent dream in which Jesus appeared wearing it led to his conversion). This relic was kept by the kings of France and taken with them on their military campaigns, and the shrine in which it was kept was also called a chapel. Later the word was used for a private shrine in a castle or house or a subsidiary worship area in a church and its officiating priest was called a chaplain. 'Chapel' is also used in Britain to designate many non-Anglican places of worship, in particular the meeting-houses of Non-Conformists and Wesleyan Methodists.

Cemeteries, Churchyards, Charnel Houses, Crypts and Catacombs
Nowadays it is commonplace for bodies to be buried in churchyards but this was not always so. The early Christians gave the name 'cemetery' (literally a 'sleeping place') to their burial grounds which were normally outside the city walls, and one of the earliest of these connected with a church were the catacombs in Rome. These formed a subterranean cemetery consisting of galleries for the dead built under the basilica of St Sebastian on the Appian Way in which Peter and Paul were supposedly buried. Smaller versions of these are known as crypts (from the Latin word meaning 'hidden'). And sometimes when burial grounds became too full the bones would be removed from the graves or tombs and stored in charnel houses (deriving from the same root as 'carnal').

Shrines and Sites of Pilgrimage. The act of pilgrimage, in which people travel to a sacred place or shrine, plays a part in many religions (as with Benares in India or Mecca). The first Christian pilgrims naturally headed towards Bethlehem and Jerusalem, especially after the building of the church of the Holy Sepulchre – allegedly over the grave of Jesus – in the reign of the Roman emperor Constantine in the 4th century. Later pilgrims visited shrines and tombs erected to saints in Rome and elsewhere, a particularly popular destination in the Middle Ages being that to James – Jesus's favourite Apostle and the first to be martyred – in Santiago de Compostela (a corruption of *Giacomopostolo* 'James the Apostle'), Spain.

three children saw a vision of the Virgin Mary repeated on the same day for six months in 1917, Lourdes in France – a mecca for invalids who take the waters – where a peasant girl called Bernadette Soubirous saw a vision of the Madonna in 1858, and Lisieux, also in France (Calvados), where there is a shrine to the young Carmelite St Thérèse who died in 1897 and was canonized in 1925. In Britain early pilgrims – such as those depicted in Chaucer's *Canterbury Tales* – visited Canterbury Cathedral and the tomb of Thomas à Becket. Another still-popular holy site is Glastonbury in Somerset where, legend has it, Joseph of Aramathea (the

Mike

rich Jew who asked the Romans for Jesus's body and the first to introduce Christianity to Britain in *c*.AD 63) brought the Holy Grail (the cup used at the Last Supper) and the spear which wounded Jesus on the cross. Joseph's staff also reputedly took root there and grew into the famous Glastonbury Thorn.

Other sites of pilgrimage include the Holy House in Loreto, Italy (allegedly the home of the Virgin Mary miraculously transported there from Nazareth in the 13th century), Fatima in Portugal where

Stained Glass and Sepulchral Art.
Decorative windows in churches, in the form of mosaics of coloured and painted glass held together by strips of lead and depicting saints and religious scenes, first became popular in about the 13th century. After designing the window as a 'cartoon' the artists would build up the mosaic piece by piece and finish off by painting details of faces etc. directly onto the coloured glass. Stained glass continued to be widely used in this way until the 18th century, and even in the 19th century artists such as Wiliam Morris still actively created new designs in this medium. Windows were also commissioned as memorials to the departed, paid for by relatives with the deceased's name usually inscribed across the bottom. Effigies of the dead, either as flat portrait brasses or as life-sized three-dimensional stone, wood or metal figures only appeared in Europe in the 11th century. They normally lay fully recumbent, with hands clasped in prayer, on stone coffins known as *sarcophagi* (Greek for 'flesh-eaters', as the flesh on the bodies inside would disappear in a very short time) and could be classified by their pose (for example a male figure with crossed legs and a scallop shell denoted a Crusader, one with his hands on his breast and with a chalice was a priest). Other monuments inside churches include inscribed wall-brasses (dating from about the 13th century) and stone or marble tablets set in the walls themselves (post-Reformation). Graveyard monuments vary enormously from urns, broken pillars, cairns and crosses to statues of angels and even complete temples.

Here lies the body
of MARY GWEN
Who died at the age
of threescore & ten
And gave to the worms
what she denied
the men

McLACHLAN

'Have one for me while you're there.'

access to any kind of musical instrumentation. Later, however, when organs were able to imitate a full orchestra, they would accompany singing both by choirs and the congregation. Singing itself, in Christian churches, derived from the kind of melodies and forms practised in Jewish temple worship and now covers a wide range for use by soloists, priests, monks and nuns, congregations and choirs. Amongst these are plainsong, chants, psalms, hymns, carols, anthems and canticles. Another form of church music is bell-ringing. In Britain the preferred method uses single-note 'chiming' bells which either ring out the hour or are used in multiple sequences as 'changes'. In Europe, by contrast, carillon or multi-note bells are used.

Organs and Church Music. The pneumatic or bellows-powered organ developed out of the earlier hydraulis invented in Greece in the 3rd century BC. Though there were professional lay organ-builders by the 12th century, it wasn't until the beginning of the 16th century that the modern pedal organ with its full range of stops, pipes and keyboards emerged. At first organ music (which was banned by the Puritans, though Cromwell himself rescued the organ from Magdalen College, Oxford, and had it installed in his residence at Hampton Court) was favoured in churches without choirs or

SPREADING THE WORD

The Universal Church

hristianity has developed in a number of different ways since the Apostles first began to spread the word of God after receiving the 'gift of tongues' – allowing them to talk to foreigners in their own languages – from the Holy Spirit at the first Pentecost following Jesus's death (Whit Sunday). The Church in all its forms was at first simply known as the 'catholic' (from the Greek for 'universal') church, but when in the 4th century the Emperor Constantine moved his capital from Rome to Byzantium (renaming it Constantinople) he divided the Roman Empire into east and west, and thereby also divided Christianity. Added to which, as Peter and Paul had worked and died in Rome an increasing number of adherents began to see Latin, rather than the original Greek, as the official language of the faith. And though the bishops of the four most powerful and populous cities of the Empire – Constantinople, Rome, Alexandria and Antioch – as well as the bishop of the holy city of Jerusalem, were at first regarded as patriarchs of equal importance in the Christian world, by degrees the bishop of Rome began to assume increasing power in the west and would eventually become known as the Pope. As a result, the Eastern Church gradually broke away until it split completely in the Great Schism of 1054, being known thereafter as the Holy Orthodox Catholic Apostolic Eastern Church (or more familiarly as the Orthodox or Eastern Church), organized on a different system under the aegis of seven patriarchs. Further redefinition came with the Reformation and the rise of churches which denied the authority of the Pope and held the Bible to be paramount. In England, this came to a head with Henry's VIII's split with Rome over the issue of his divorce from Katherine of Aragon and the foundation of the Church of England (still essentially Catholic in nature at this point, though with Henry rather than the Pope as its head). The Anglican Church was not described as 'Protestant' (i.e., protesting against the Pope etc.) until 1607, followers at first calling themselves *evangelici.* The Church of England was one of four Protestant Churches, the others being the Reformed Church (based on the works of the French-born Swiss theologian John

Calvin) – which, as Presbyterianism, was very influential in Scotland (via Calvin's pupil John Knox) and to a lesser extent in England; the Lutheran Church (based on the works of the German Martin Luther); and the Moravian Church (based on the work of Wycliff's pupil John Hus who came from Moravia and was to influence Methodism). The Protestant churches have since spawned a number of sub-groups. Some are independent churches with just one branch, while others have become recognized denominations such as Baptists, Congregationalists, Methodists, Assemblies of God and the Vineyard Churches.

'It's one of those moderate groups!'

Missionaries. Unlike some other religions in which converting of disbelievers is not a part, Jesus specifically asked his Apostles to go out into the world and preach his message. He had said, 'Go therefore and make disciples of all nations, baptizing them in the name of the Father and of the Son and of the Holy Spirit, teaching them to observe all that I have commanded you.' However, at first this was only taken to apply to Jews of all nations as none, not even Peter, had thought that Christianity was intended for uncircumcised Gentiles and heathens. As such, the 12 Apostles divided up their areas of responsibility and became evangelists (spreaders of good news). The Apostles were thus the first ever missionaries and the story of their work is recounted in the Acts of the Apostles. The second half of Acts is devoted to Paul, the greatest of the biblical missionaries. Originally named Saul and of the tribe of Benjamin (Jacob's youngest son), he had in fact studied as a Pharisee (the strictest of the three Jewish sects, the others being the Sadducees and the Essenes) and had not only actively persecuted Christians but had been at the stoning of Stephen, the first Christian martyr. However, on the way from Jerusalem to arrest a Christian colony in Damascus one day he was blinded by a holy light, healed by the Damascan Christian Ananias, and was converted, taking the name of Paul (Paulos being the Greek equivalent of the Hebrew Saul). Though he had not known Jesus personally like the other 12, Paul has been accepted as a *de facto* Apostle and, accompanied by Barnabas, travelled extensively in Asia Minor, and visited all the major Greek cities in the Mediterranean area promoting Christianity, especially to the Gentiles. Most of the epistles of the New Testament – addressed to local bishops or inhabitants – are by Paul. He was beheaded in Rome in AD 66 during Nero's purges following the Great Fire which destroyed part of the city and was blamed on the Christians (Peter also died in the purges). During the reign of Constantine, the Roman Empire became increasingly tolerant and by *c*.AD 400 Christianity had become the official religion. However, there were still outposts of paganism and St Patrick (Ireland), St Columba (Scotland), St Augustine (England) and St Boniface (Germany) were some of the notable missionaries who carried the Pope's message in the following years. Later still came the Society of Jesus (the Jesuits) and such Protestant missionary soceties as SPCK – the Society for Promoting Christian Knowledge – (1698), the London

Missionary Society (1795), the Church Missionary Society (1799) and the Wesleyan Methodist Missionary Society (1813). All of these, and many more, travelled the world – especially South America and Africa – trying to convert indigenous peoples from their traditional religions to Christianity. In modern times some evangelists have also broadcast on TV and radio while others have drawn huge crowds as they practised faith-healing.

The Puritan Movement. The term 'Puritan' was originally a derogatory description given to a group of 'purist' Anglican Protestants who were very much in evidence in England for about 100 years from the beginning of the reign of Elizabeth I until the Restoration of the Monarchy under Charles II in 1660. Basically Calvinist in belief, and advocating the Bible as the only true source of Christian faith and conduct, the more right-wing Puritans were Presbyterians while the left-wing ones were Independents (who held local churches to be sovereign and owed no allegiance to other churches or organizations). Severe in their own personal deportment, they censured licentiousness and frivolity in others – such as dancing and the theatre – and also banned organs in churches, ministerial vestments, church furnishings and statuary etc. The English Civil War was essentially a Puritan revolution against the by then Catholic monarchy and was supported by Parliament and the Parliamentary Armies (Roundheads) under Oliver Cromwell against Charles I and his Royalist forces (Cavaliers). The Pilgrim Fathers who settled the first permanent colony in what would become the USA in 1620 were Puritans.

'I've been mugged...!'

Crusaders. In the Middle Ages the pilgrim route to the Holy Sepulchre at Jerusalem was under constant threat from Muslim forces and, as a result, Pope Urban II suggested that western European troops, led by a papal legate, should be sent in the name of Christianity to safeguard access to the shrine. This was the First Crusade of 1095. A further seven major crusades followed until 1303 and minor ones continued until the mid-15th century. Richard I ('the Lionheart') of England led the Third Crusade, together with King Philip Augustus of France and the German King and Holy Roman Emperor Frederick I ('Barbarossa' – or Redbeard), against the Muslim ruler Saladin. Not all the Crusades were successful, however, and in many cases the Crusaders' motivation seemed to have more to do with plunder than religion. The word 'Crusader' derives from the fact that the Christian soldiers wore crosses (Latin *crux*) on their tunics which were differently coloured according to their country of origin (England wore white tunics, France red, Italy blue etc.).

'I'm alive really – I got this at Ye Jolly Saracen Joke Shoppe . . . !'

The Gideon Bible. The Gideons – more correctly the Christian Commercial Men's Association – were founded in Wisconsin, USA, in 1899 by three travelling businessmen. Taking their shortened name from the Israelite 'judge' or leader who (according to Judges Chapter VII) successfully repulsed the invading Midianite army in a heroic battle, the Gideons try to lead people to Christianity by putting Bibles in hotel rooms, hospitals, prisons, schools etc.

Jehovah's Witnesses. Known at first as International Bible Students, the Jehovah's Witness movement was founded in 1872 by Charles Taze Russell in Philadephia, USA. They don't recognize Jesus as divine (though they believe he was an agent of God), seeing only Jehovah as the supreme being. In addition they don't believe in Hell, think Roman Catholics and Protestants have been misguided by Satan and disapprove of divorce, tobacco and alcohol. However, they are firm adherents of the doctrine of baptism by total immersion. Because they only recognize the authority of Jehovah, they refuse to salute national flags or perform military service. Their magazine is called the *Watchtower*.

'We're Jehovah's Waitresses . . .'

'Armageddon's coming next week – do we buy the magazine?'

The Mormons. The Church of Jesus of Latter-Day Saints – commonly known as The Mormons – was founded by Joseph Smith in 1830. Ten years earlier, aged 14, Smith had witnessed a vision of God and Jesus in the woods near the family home in Vermont and then in 1823 an ancient American Indian prophet of Israelite origin (the 10 Lost Tribes having allegedly found their way to the USA) called Moroni had appeared to him and directed him to hidden golden plates on which were inscribed ancient scriptures and history. In 1827 Smith found the plates and translated them as *The Book of Mormon* (Mormon being the name of an American Indian prophet who had made an abstract of earlier plates). After Smith was murdered by a mob in 1844 the movement fled from their base in Nauvoo, Illinois, and, led by their new leader Brigham Young, trekked 1000 miles to the Promised Land on the Great Salt Lake (then outside of the USA) and established what was to become Salt Lake City, which became part of the USA (as Utah) in 1896. Their holy books comprise the Bible, *The Book of Mormon*, *Doctrine and Covenants* (revelations of Joseph Smith) and *The Pearl of Great Price* (alleged revelations and writings of Moses and Abraham not included in the Bible). Members abstain from alcohol, tobacco, coffee and tea and were at one time in favour of polygamy (this practice was renounced in 1890).

'If I joined, how many wives could I have?'

The Salvation Army. Founded in Whitechapel, London, in 1865 by former Methodist minister William Booth, the Salvation Army was originally called the Christian Mission but adopted its more familiar title in 1878. An evangelical movement, the Salvation Army, which is organized on military lines (William Booth was its first General) and dresses its members in uniform, works to improve the lot of the disadvantaged in society, hoping that by so helping them they will be better able to understand the Christian message. Its activities include the running of rehabilitation centres, night-shelters and clinics. Brass bands playing hymns and open-air services are a distinctive mark of the Salvation Army. Its motto is 'Through Blood and Fire' and its newspaper is called the *War Cry*.

'He's easing his son into the business...'